MISSION: FREEDOM

A Combat Veteran's Battle Plan to Destroy PTSD and Live Free

DAVID SHOUP

DEDICATION

This book—and everything in it: its strategies, its concepts, its approaches and systems—is all dedicated to my brothers in arms. To those who fought battles not only on the field, but within their own minds. To those who have been fighting with inner demons for years, desperately wanting relief. This work is dedicated to all those who believe they cannot heal.

It is dedicated to all those who have gone in support and in defense of our great nation and came home with scars—some visible, others not. To those who returned home changed, who have never seen the world the same again, who feel misunderstood in their homes by their families, friends, and communities. To those who want to crush PTSD and experience freedom from all of its symptoms once and for all—this work is for you.

It's for the brave men and women I served alongside who lost their battles with their inner demons, who desperately wanted help, service, and healing, but never got what they needed in time.

It's for all those who want life to be different, who want hope and freedom from the unbearable weight of the burdens they carry every single day.

This book is for you. May these words free you from the past like they did for me, and may you discover that healing is closer than you ever imagined.

CONTENTS

ACKNOWLEDGMENTS

First and foremost, I want to thank my loving wife for all the nights she spent holding my hand on the floor of our bedroom as I struggled, for being my partner through this and supporting me through my journey in obtaining the freedom that I now have. Without her, this would not have happened. We are partners in life, in business, and in this mission.

I'd also like to thank my children who were there with me through the darkness and the struggles. Though they may not have understood what was happening and why Daddy spent so much time alone, I have incredible appreciation and gratitude for my family.

I'd also like to thank my parents. Thank you for laying the foundation that made this possible. You taught me resilience, grit, and the value of hard work even when life was anything but easy. The lessons forged in those early years became the base that shaped who I am today. I honor you both for your sacrifices, your perseverance, and the love—spoken and unspoken—that gave me the strength to become the man I was meant to be.

I'd also like to acknowledge and thank Tony Robbins. It was at his event called *Date With Destiny* in 2023, where I learned critical strategies that I was able to take and apply to my PTSD. He helped me understand that anything can be changed and healed—even my very identity and the reality that I see. I learned numerous techniques and strategies during my time with him, which brought significant value to my healing journey.

I'd also like to thank my Lord God, Jesus Christ. For saving me, healing me, and giving me access to all these life-saving tools that I now share with you.

I'd also like to thank RJon Robbins, Chief Executive Officer of *How to Manage a Small Law Firm*. While his primary focus was teaching me how to run our law firms, he also worked with me to understand my trauma, my symptoms, and how to build our businesses around them. Thank you for everything that you did.

I'd also like to thank an employee of RJon Robbins, Erica Ferenzi, who coached me on a fateful Mastermind in 2019. She helped me see that I didn't have to continue to "white knuckle" through each day or persevere through so much pain; I could ask for help. This was the first day of my healing journey and I'm grateful for our time together. She told me, "David, you're a lion, but you see yourself as an Itty Bitty Kitty". This has stuck with me to this day and became a fundamental principle for the work I do in my own life and offer in this book: How you perceive yourself is how you are. Thank you for this lesson.

I'd finally like to thank my therapist, Ashlee Fisher, for all the years we spent together on "Team David." She was absolutely critical in helping me free myself from my greatest enemy. She was there from the beginning of my journey through to our final call when I told her that I was free and had never felt better in my entire life. Thank you for your unwavering commitment to my healing and the absolute freedom that I now enjoy. I will be forever grateful for our time together.

INTRODUCTION

I grew up in the Midwest. Before the Marines, I was a lighthearted, hopeful person. I thought I'd live a "normal" life—committed to pursuing a career as a minister for my church. Then September 11th, 2001 changed everything. I felt the fire to serve, to fight for something bigger than myself. My father taught me that military service was the greatest honor one could attain. So, naturally, I felt called even though no one in my family had served before. I decided to enlist in the Marine Corps infantry for one simple reason: freedom wasn't free and our great nation was being attacked. I longed for the structure and discipline that I believed the Marine Corps would give me. I sought a stronger version of myself—one who belonged to something meaningful.

In some ways, it did make me stronger. But in most ways, combat broke me. Iraq left marks no one could see—snipers, IEDs, and the constant tension of never knowing if we would return to our forward operating base. Before every patrol I would bow my head and go to my knees, seeking God's protection.

The reality is: the man who left for Iraq was not the man who returned. I struggled with symptoms I didn't even have names for yet. At the time, I didn't even know what PTSD was, much less that I was living with it. No one taught us how to recognize it or even navigate it.

The reality is: PTSD nearly took everything from me—my marriage, my career, even my life. It seemed like danger lurked behind every corner and shadow. I lived with constant restlessness, flashbacks, suicidal thoughts, and depressive episodes.

When I came home, I couldn't sit with my wife on the couch without feeling miles away. Most nights, I chose the floor over the bed because sleep never came easy—nightmares yanked me back to Iraq until I woke up drenched in sweat. I snapped at my wife over nothing. I pulled away from friends because crowds felt like ambushes. A simple trip to the store was a mission—every exit mapped, every person scanned, every noise a threat. I would sit wide awake in bed at every noise, planning for an intruder that was never there.

At work, my focus shattered. I'd stare at a screen for hours, body rigid, mind racing, waiting for something I couldn't name. I felt gripped by anxiety every minute of every day. My temper made me unpredictable. My silence made me unreachable. I felt like I was failing at everything: failing my wife, failing my future, failing myself.

And worse still—I believed there was nothing I could do about it. I was told that *this is how life is now*. This belief brought me to my breaking point. For me, it wasn't one big explosion. It was a death by a thousand cuts. Night after sleepless night, I would wake up soaked in sweat, fists clenched and heart pounding. I felt ashamed seeing my wife or kids' faces when I snapped at them for no reason, the guilt of knowing I was physically home but emotionally gone, like a ghost haunting my own life. Living like this for years without relief, I began to ponder how much longer I could go on and whether this was really worth the battle anymore. I felt trapped in a prison I couldn't escape, chained by rage, fear, and exhaustion.

"If this is life now, why keep going?"

I didn't want to die, but I didn't know how to live. This was the edge—the darkest place I had ever been.

It was from this place that I finally decided that I had had enough and needed help. And so my 5½-year-long war against PTSD started.

Along the way, I came to learn a fundamental truth that changed everything: "it doesn't have to be this way." I could be free—not just coping or managing—but *free*. I could truly rid myself of these symptoms for the rest of my life. It was from this place of hard-won freedom that I built the strategies, systems, and techniques that I teach in this book and in my various programs.

I teach this material because I feel called to share my journey—what I endured and the struggles I overcame on my way to complete freedom from my greatest adversary. I teach it because I've been there, I've done that, I've been in the darkness, and I conquered my pain. I did this, and you can do this too. That's why I decided to make this my mission in life: to teach as many combat veterans as I possibly can about three simple truths: (1) You are not broken; (2) Life does not have to be this way; and (3) You can be free whenever you so choose.

This will not be easy. In fact, this may be the most difficult battle that you'll ever fight. But know this: freedom from your past is possible. You can free yourself from your burdens and the weight you're carrying, from the pain that you feel. You can live a life of abundance, joy, happiness, and peace.

The choice is yours. I invite you to take this journey with me to learn what I've learned and do what I did so you can reclaim your best life—for you, your children, and your family. But it all comes down to you and your decision to heal.

It's your time now. Combat has already cost you enough—don't let it take everything. Freedom is rightfully yours.

PART I

MISSION BRIEFING (PREPARATION)

CHAPTER 1

THE LINE OF DEPARTURE

THE BATTLEFIELD

Welcome to the beginning of the rest of your life. And no—I don't think I'm being overly dramatic. What you're about to embark on could save your life and completely change its outcome, including the connection you have with your family, your children, your career, and your business. Every aspect of your life is contingent on this journey. How you interact with the world depends on your physical and mental health, your mindset, and how you walk through post-traumatic stress. And that's exactly what we're dealing with here.

Our target is PTSD—post-traumatic stress disorder. This is the greatest enemy our veteran community faces today. Between 2008 and 2013, more than 500,000 veterans were treated for PTSD by the VA,[1] and roughly 30,000 veterans have died by suicide since 9/11—four times

---

1. U.S. Department of Veterans Affairs. (n.d.). *Overview of VA Research on Posttraumatic Stress Disorder (PTSD).* VA Research and Development. *https://www.research.va.gov/topics/ptsd.cfm*

more than were killed in combat over the same period.[2] Twenty-five percent of the veterans who served in Operation Iraqi Freedom and Operation Enduring Freedom will develop post-traumatic stress,[3] and every single day, 18 veterans commit suicide,[4] largely due to untreated PTSD.

PTSD is not just a statistic—it's our enemy. It's the killer we're going to destroy. And mark my words: by the end of this journey, you will have destroyed post-traumatic stress. You will have taken back ground and reclaimed your life and your God-given freedom. This is a process, so it doesn't matter where you are along this journey. It just matters that you start and that you employ the tools I'm going to teach you.

You can experience freedom from the anxiety, depression, hypervigilance, obsessive anger, doubt, guilt, and shame that keep you tied to the past. I know you may be thinking: *What if I can't get better? What if nothing changes? I can't keep doing this!* I get it. I was there. In 2019, I knew nothing about these tools. All I knew was that I wanted the pain to end. I wanted relief. I wanted hope that I could change.

This is what brought me to my therapist for the first time. When I finally walked into her office, it wasn't because I believed I needed therapy. It was because I had hit a wall. The constant anxiety, sleepless nights, and relentless pain had finally pushed me past my breaking point, and I couldn't take it anymore. I had joined a mastermind group with a coach hoping for relief, and it was that process that made me realize I needed to talk to someone. I remember what the coach said to me one day: "David... you need help."

2. Suitt, T. H. III. (2021, June 21). *High suicide rates among United States service members and veterans of the post-9/11 wars.* Costs of War, Boston University. https://watson.brown.edu/costsofwar/papers/2021/Suicides

3. Seal, K. H., Bertenthal, D., Miner, C. R., Sen, S., & Marmar, C. (2007). Mental health disorders and diagnoses in a cohort of 103,788 veterans returning from Iraq and Afghanistan seen at Department of Veterans Affairs facilities. *Archives of Internal Medicine, 167*(5), 476–82.

4. Everytown for Gun Safety Support Fund. (2025). *Those Who Serve: Addressing Firearm Suicide Among Military Veterans.* Everytown Research & Policy. https://everytownresearch.org/report/those-who-serve/

Still, even then, I didn't know I had PTSD. I thought this was just what it meant to be a veteran who had seen combat—that the rage, hypervigilance, and exhaustion were simply part of the deal. Sitting in that chair, I told her I probably just needed a couple of sessions, a quick tune-up for my anxiety, and then I'd be fine. The truth was I was still in denial, blind to how severe my symptoms really were, and resisting the possibility that something much bigger was going on. But thank God I did seek her out... because this was the start of my healing journey.

This is where you must start as well: assessing your own reality and knowing where you stand. You must assess where you are right now, who you're showing up as in your life, and what you're doing regularly. If you're going to use a map, you must first know where you are. Without this information, everything else is useless. That is why I'm going to give you homework assignments throughout the book to really drive these lessons home. While we're doing the work together, you *must* apply what you learn. You must take this seriously if you want real results.

Another note for you: I am going to teach you with lots of repetition. Throughout my journey, I was taught that repetition is the mother of all mastery, and I will deploy the same approach with you. I am going to give you lessons, concepts, and assignments over and over again to drive home the fundamental concepts and principles you will learn here. Then you must apply them and do the work over and over again until your PTSD is completely destroyed. But it will take the repetition that I've laid out in this book—so expect it.

To help you apply what you're learning, visit *www.WarriorsAwakening. com/free-resources* for free resources you can use when completing your assignments, as well as diagrams and videos to coach you through this process. Use them as much or as little as you like—but use them. Download the journal prompts and complete them. The more you physically write this stuff out and do the work, the better your outcome will be.

ASSIGNMENT 1: Understand your reality. Ask yourself:

- Where are you in life?

- Who have you become?

- What are your dominant thoughts, your emotions, and your feelings?

- What do your relationships look like?

- Who do you see yourself as?

I am _____.

Fill in the blank. Who are you? Define yourself as you stand here today. Now understand that this is not where you're going to be by the end of this book. This is not how this ends for you, but you need to understand who you define yourself as today—what emotions, thoughts, feelings, and sensations race through your body every single day—so you can locate yourself on the map. This is where you start.

Face the truth, because it will set you free. If you lie to yourself, cover up what's really going on, or ignore the reality of your situation and what you're facing now, you will quit. You will sabotage your progress and never experience full healing, and I know that's not what you want. You want to be free. You want a life that doesn't look and feel this way.

Opening this book was your first step. From one combat veteran to another, know this: this will be a long road, but your life doesn't have to stay this way. If you commit to using these strategies, you will be free.

DEFINING THE TARGET

Now it's time to determine what you're fighting for. Remember, the map is only useful if you know where you're starting from and what the destination is. You need to determine what you want out of your life at this moment. So let's narrow this down a little bit. What do you want out of this experience and our journey together? Relief? Hope? Peace? Better relationships? What is your current focus?

This is your journey and you must choose your target. You're in charge. I will be here to coach you and guide you through the strategies and pitfalls. But you have to define the result. You have to know where you want to go, even if it's just, "I want to feel hope."

You'll experience relief if you're willing to put in the work and commit yourself to this process. You're a combat veteran of the United States military. You know how to put in the work.

I know what you're thinking right now. *What if I can't do this? What if it's too much? What if digging into this pain just makes it worse?* Maybe you've already told yourself you don't have the time, or that you've survived this long so you don't need to stir it up. Maybe you're afraid that if you really open this door, you won't be able to shut it again. I get it—I had all those same fears. But that thinking is just resistance trying to keep you stuck where you are. You've faced firefights, deployments, and battles most people could never imagine. You've already proven you can endure hell and come out alive. Compared to that, this is a different kind of fight, but it's the most important one of your life. Lean into the discomfort. Push through the fear. Apply the same strength, focus, and determination that got you this far. Victory is on the other side, and you will never regret fighting for it.

ASSIGNMENT 2: Time to assess the satisfaction you currently feel with where you are. Ask yourself:

- Am I satisfied with where I am right now?
- Am I satisfied with how I feel?
- Am I satisfied with who I am?

If the answer to these questions is no, then first consider: why do you feel unsatisfied? Get as clear as possible. Then, define what you *do* want. Where *do* you want to be? What *do* you want to feel? Close your eyes and visualize your ideal life. Visualize who you'll be at the end of this journey. Visualize your relationships. How do you want to connect with your spouse? How do you want to connect with your children? Refer back to the previous section's assignment as you do this exercise.

Now reflect on the emotions you feel while visualizing each of these scenarios. What is your dominant emotion? I started with a simple goal: I just wanted relief from the pain I felt every single day. That small flicker of hope was enough to keep me moving forward. What do you want from your life at the end of our time together? Write down your answer. This is your destination. I want you to *see* this person in your mind, because this is the person that you will become.

Some of you may not have done this kind of exercise before, but consider that this is the same practice that worked so well for you during service: to focus on a clear mission. It's fairly simple, without a target, you can't hit the bullseye. In my various businesses, the clearer I got on where I was going, the more successful I was. My superpower is perseverance and unwavering focus. When I clearly set my goals and targets, I smash them every time.

IDENTIFYING THE OBSTACLES

The next step in this battle is getting clear about what you want to change. A broad vision isn't enough—you need specific targets; concrete pieces of the puzzle. However, to build some momentum, I want you to start with a general approach. We will get specific later.

ASSIGNMENT 3: When you look at your life:

- What do you want to change?
- What really *needs* to change?

To do this, think about your life in its entirety. An example could be: "I am unhappy about the quality of my relationships. At this point in my life, I don't feel close to anyone. I really want to be closer to my family." Reflect on what you want and journal about it now.

Once you reflect on the big thing you want to change in your life, you need to know what is keeping you stuck, what is keeping you imprisoned and away from your ideal life and the outcome you want.

To do this, you need to understand your enemy. What is it that keeps you from healing? Maybe it's sensations like guilt, fear, anxiety, panic attacks, or dissociation. Whatever it is, you need to name it. But before you can do that, you need to understand what I mean by "sensations."

A sensation is what your body feels when PTSD is triggered. It's the pounding heart, the sweat on your palms, the knot in your gut, the tightness in your chest, the shaking in your hands, or the sudden rush of adrenaline that makes you feel like you're back in the fight. These sensations come from your nervous system. When a noise, a smell, a sight—or anything that reminds your subconscious of combat—hits you, it can fire up your sympathetic nervous system (your fight-or-flight response). Your body reacts as if you're in danger, even if you're completely safe. That's what leads to flashbacks, panic attacks, or the overwhelming feeling that you can't breathe.

Here's the key: knowing this gives you power. These reactions are not proof that you're broken. They're simply your body trying to protect you. Once you see that these sensations are signals, rather than as something that is wrong with you, you can learn to rewire them. This will be a core part of our work together. And while sensations are strong, your biggest enemy isn't the sensations themselves, it's resistance—your resistance to change and your brain's desire to keep you exactly where you are now.

This journey is going to challenge your beliefs, forcing you to change old habits and disrupt old routines. You're going to be rewriting your very identity, and bringing yourself from the "known" to the "unknown." This will trigger your brain and your entire nervous system to feel immense discomfort, because where you are feels "safe" to your brain, even though it will cause you incredible damage if you remain here. Your brain will trigger a sensation of "fear" to try and keep you safe. Recognize it. Understand it. Proceed anyways.

Take this to heart now: the biggest opposition here is not actually the anxiety, guilt, or fear you feel. Those are the sensations that your brain is creating. Your biggest opposition is staying stuck and bowing to the resistance that your brain creates to keep you "safe," even to your own destruction. You know what's behind you. You don't know what's ahead.

So until you condition yourself to accept that difficulty is something to treasure (because it means you're growing), you're going to hit resistance over and over again. And if you allow resistance to stop you, you will reinforce it and make it much more likely to happen again. Never bow to the fear your brain creates. It is actually a signal to proceed. Stand your ground.

Here's the first truth bomb that will piss some of you off (which by the way I am completely okay with because I am here to help you grow, not make you feel comfortable):

Most of you are in a prison. A prison that traps you and enslaves you. But this prison? You built it. Your brain built these walls, and your thoughts and beliefs reinforced them. You're living inside a jail cell that you created.

But the good news is that once you accept this truth, you'll understand the power you have to set yourself free. If this is your prison, then you are the warden. You're in charge. You can leave this prison whenever you want.

This should give you incredible hope. This realization helped to set me free. The only thing that was standing in the way of my absolute and total freedom was *me*. My sensations, my feelings, my thoughts—these were all things that my body was creating. It was internal, not external, and if it was created, it could be destroyed.

Once I had my eye on my target, I could aim.

So build your target. What obstacles are standing in your way? What do you need to get rid of?

TIME TO CONSTRUCT YOUR BATTLE BOARD

Now, before we proceed, I want you to add a powerful tool to your strategies that I will call your "Battle Board." Your central Battle Board—a/k/a a vision board—is going to grow with you as you move through this book. This isn't arts and crafts; it's your war map. Every exercise we do—your eulogy, your outcome, your why—will produce raw power you don't want to lose in a pile of papers. Take the most critical words or images from each exercise and add them to this board. By the end of this book, you'll have a single, complete visual battle plan for your freedom—a board that reminds you daily who you are becoming, what you're fighting for, and why you'll never quit.

NAMING THE ENEMY

Anxiety, depression, fear, anger. These are all just sensations you have—and they matter, but there are bigger opponents than these. One of your biggest targets will be your inner demons.

These are the voices and shadows that follow you, and they can be compelling. They may speak to you in a voice of despair, and may even sound like someone you know. They may speak to you in your own voice or the voice of a fallen comrade begging you to save them. Perhaps your darkness manifests as suicidal thoughts, or maybe you black out or are overcome with rage. You need to look these demons in the eye and understand them, because they are powerful.

These inner demons are fed by what you consume. And I don't just mean what you eat or drink. I mean the beliefs you ruminate on, the stories you tell yourself, and the meaning you attach to what has happened to you. These are your self-defeating beliefs—the internal lies that say, *I'm broken. I'll never get better. I'm a burden to my family.* Every time you feed these beliefs, your demons grow stronger. They chain you to your past, rob you of hope, and make healing feel impossible.

This matters because until you expose these lies for what they are, you'll never gain control of the fight. PTSD is not just about what happened to you—it's about the meaning you attach to it and the beliefs you allow to take root. What do you tolerate within your own mind? If you want freedom, you must starve the demons and feed the truth. That starts with recognizing that your beliefs either build your prison, or hand you the key to walk out.

So here's your next assignment: it's time to wage the war against your inner demons.

ASSIGNMENT 4: Identify your inner demons and your darkness.

Get really clear about what you are tolerating within you. Whatever comes to your mind, I want you to write it down. Then do the following:

- List your inner demons, even if it's just by describing them.
- Next, name them. Even if it is just the "Annoying One" or something equally simple. This will help you recognize them when they approach. I'll teach you how to handle them, but for now, start small.
- Next, identify what triggers them. Perhaps it's a sound, like the washing machine firing off, a certain word, or even a tone of voice. Anything that brings them forth, write it down.

You will now have a working list of your inner demons—what they are and when they approach. For now, just see them and understand them. Don't worry about crushing them… yet. That will come later.

At this point, some of you may be thinking that it's safer to retreat—to avoid or numb what needs to be faced. This will result in you never healing. Nothing short of their pure annihilation will set you free.

When I first faced my demons, I was brought to my knees. I had a complete break from reality, and it felt like I was literally losing my own mind. I heard guns loading, vehicles that approached were all holding terrorists, and even complete strangers were enemies. The depression was crushing—I couldn't get out of bed, couldn't look my wife in the eye, and didn't even recognize myself. Suicidal thoughts circled me like vultures, and I felt powerless to stop them. Every ounce of strength I had on the battlefield seemed gone, and I couldn't do the simplest things in daily life. I ended up checking myself into two back-to-back intensive outpatient clinics at the local VA hospital. During my time there, even the simplest tasks—like finishing a puzzle—were overwhelming. I felt stripped of everything I thought I was—my pride, my toughness, my ability to "hold it together."

That's why when you say, *David, I feel like I'm on the edge,* I don't just hear you—I feel you, because I was you. I know the weight of that darkness. I walked through that valley where hope felt empty and life felt like a fight I couldn't win. Know this: it doesn't have to be this way. If I can come back from that pit, so can you.

YOUR RULES OF ENGAGEMENT

Before we go any farther, we need to establish our Rules of Engagement. Every combat zone that we entered into when we were on active duty had rules we needed to follow to stay alive. My own therapist laid down these rules for me on Day One and it probably saved my life.

The number one rule when you're embarking on this journey, gentlemen, is safety. **Rule #1: Safety is always first.**

If at any point you feel that your safety is at risk, I want you to put down this book. Call your therapist, psychiatrist, or your spouse. If that doesn't work, call 911. Seek help immediately. You can't heal if you're hurt or dead. This is your instruction, your order from me to you. Don't be afraid to lose your job. Don't be afraid to scare your family by letting them know that you're hurting, that you can't hide this anymore. By continuing to hide this, you will not heal. And if you don't heal, you'll lose everything you've been afraid to risk in the first place. So yes, there are risks to reaching out. But safety first.

Additionally, I recommend that every single person reading this find a good therapist that can help you through this journey. Go to *www. WarriorsAwakening.com/free-resources* or scan the QR code in the back of this book to find a guide on how to choose the right therapist and more information about the techniques I will discuss later. Keep it handy from the beginning—you may need it sooner than you think.

Next up is **Rule #2: Take your time.** Go at your own pace, taking as much or as little time as you need. When I worked through this process myself, it took me days to read a few pages of my PTSD workbooks because of how triggered I got each time, and that's okay. You can expect the same if you struggle with flashbacks, hypervigilance, or intense anxiety.

There are no time restraints for doing this work, but that doesn't mean you should resort to patterns of avoidance when it gets challenging. If you get triggered and you need to take a few minutes to cope, take that time to calm yourself using your tools. Then return to the task at hand and continue. While you will learn extensive coping strategies during our time together, let me give you one now: the power of your breath.

Sit in a firm chair with your feet flat on the ground. Place your hands comfortably on your knees with your palms up, hands relaxed, and eyes closed. Take a full, deep breath in for seven to 10 seconds. Imagine cool, deep blue light filling your chest as you take your air in. Then hold the breath for four to five seconds and imagine the light filling your body. Then start to slowly exhale for another seven to 10 seconds and imagine the light exiting your body from your chest and hands. Hold there for another four to five seconds and then repeat. You can even say, "I am calm" or simply "calm" through this process. At a minimum, think the words in your mind. This process will calm your nervous system within a matter of minutes.

A core tenet of coping is that you must keep coping until your symptoms return to zero without exception. Take your breaks, then return to the fight.

Rule #3: Always do your work in the same place every day, and stick to this. This will condition your brain to see that space as a healing zone. I also recommend that you do your healing work at the same time every day whenever possible. Your body loves patterns and consistency, so your body should know when it's time to work on freedom just like it knows when it's time to sleep. For those of you that have children, you know exactly what I'm talking about. Kids thrive on routines—and so does your nervous system. By setting up schedules for yourself in certain locations, you'll speed up the process and make it more effective, which will ultimately help you stay the course. In combat you learned when to fight, and now you're learning when to stop.

Before we continue, I want to repeat **Rule #1: Safety First.** Reach out for help if you believe you're at risk. Staying alive is your priority.

THERE'S NO MAGIC PILL

I need to give this next point to you straight: Your healing is your responsibility. As your leader on this journey, I will not sugarcoat things, and I sure as hell am not going to lie to you. I will teach you what you need to know, and in the order you need to know it. I will give you the work that you need to do and the strategies to deploy. **But you need to customize these strategies for yourself because your**

symptoms are unique to you. Your trauma is different to mine. This is your journey, and you're in charge.

You must remember that your symptoms will not go away on their own. This will never get better if you don't take effective action. There's no magic pill, no secret sauce that will erase what you've been through.

You can't heal if you're living in denial—a false reality with your head up your ass. You need to face the truth. A wound on your body, like a cut, will heal over time; your body is designed to do that. But trauma doesn't play by those rules. It buries itself deep. That's why years after combat, veterans with PTSD can start crying out of nowhere. Seeing or hearing a trigger from years before can cause you to jump out of your chair. Trauma does not care about time. The body never forgets what it experiences—unless it is retrained to associate something different with what occurred in the past.

Your brain was built for survival. When you face danger, your nervous system stores the sights, sounds, and sensations so it can warn you next time. It's an evolutionary function—designed to keep you from repeating a scenario that almost killed you. But combat doesn't just give you one near-death moment, it floods you with repeated exposure to danger every single day. That survival system gets set on fire, and it doesn't shut off when you come home. What was meant to keep you alive on the battlefield is now misfiring in civilian life. That's why understanding and rewiring this response is critical to healing.

At the start of my journey, I was told during a combat veteran support group that this was just the way life was going to be for me from then on. "You'll be dealing with these symptoms for the rest of your life." What they forgot to add was, "… without effective action being taken." Unfortunately, veterans are told this every day across our nation from the VA and various other support groups. These groups do not know any other reality. Sadly, this does so much damage to our war heroes, leading veterans to simply believe, as I did, that nothing will ever change.

Contrary to what I know many of you have heard, we can destroy our PTSD and live freely whenever we so choose. But know this: Without deploying the tools laid out in this book, you will have PTSD for the rest of your life. Your body, your brain, and your nervous system will keep their conditioning forever. By deploying these strategies with intense focus and commitment, I crushed my symptoms, and I know you can too.

CHAPTER 2

LOCKING IN THE WARRIOR'S MINDSET

FRAME THE MISSION

Let's return to the most important thing for you right now: Your defined outcome. To effectively obtain your outcome, you need to see it clearly in your mind. This time, you need to get very specific. You have a series of general outcomes that you want; now I want you to get as granular as possible. Close your eyes and *see* a specific outcome in your mind. It should be objective, clear, and you should have clear criteria for success, so you know exactly when you've achieved it—nothing vague or unclear.

ASSIGNMENT 5: Time to define your specific targets that you will achieve, no matter what.

Visualize it first, then write down:

- What is going to change? What will you have or obtain? (Think of your body, your finances, your relationships, your job or business—make it clear.)

- What will you achieve?
- What will you no longer tolerate?
- Who will you become?

Caution: Do not make your target to "feel better" or be "further along." This is not specific, not objective, and not helpful right now. If you don't aim at a bullseye, I guarantee you won't hit it. Clarity is power.

Let's also build some leverage for yourself with your targets.

- How will you feel when you reach your goal and hit all the targets you set for yourself?
- What will you think when you hit your goal?

Feel the excitement and joy as you envision complete mission accomplishment. Your relationships have been enhanced, your finances have substantially improved, your business is revamped, your emotions are under control and your PTSD is completely gone. The more vivid the picture, the stronger your leverage will be. Clear target, clear strategy, clear results.

You'll notice that you are planning for where you are "going." But to plan for this new direction in your life, you need to understand exactly where you "are" now. Take some time now and assess:

- Where am I right now?
- What do I feel?
- What do I regularly experience?
- What am I consistently receiving with my current experiences?

This will help you clarify exactly where you are, what you are doing, and what you are achieving *currently*, because a direction and a related objective is only helpful if you know exactly where you are and precisely what it is you are aiming for.

Don't worry about the "how" for now. Don't worry if it seems impossible. I'll take you there, and you will learn all the strategies you need to make it happen. Right now, I want you to nail down the "what."

In 2023, after five years of fighting the same battles and getting nowhere, I reached a point when I got sick of what was happening in my life. When I got to my first Tony Robbins event called *Date With Destiny*, I was ready for change.

I couldn't tolerate it anymore. I wasn't getting any better. Maybe some of you can identify with this right now. I realized, at that moment, that I was heading to my own death, physically and emotionally. And if you're emotionally dead, you're a walking corpse. Your relationships are destroyed, all business opportunities are lost, and your children don't even know who you are anymore.

This is and was not acceptable, so I decided to take action. I wasn't going to let anything stop me.

The next assignment will help you figure out exactly what you're going to change, where you are, and where you're going to go instead. You're going to write your own eulogy. If you want to use my prompt to help you get started, visit the resource page, *www.WarriorsAwakening.com/free-resources*, and download it now. On the resource page you'll find templates, prompts, and other tools to help you do these exercises—so take advantage of it.

ASSIGNMENT 6: Writing your eulogy.

Imagine you died of a sudden heart attack 20 minutes from now. What will be said about you at your funeral? Write it on a piece of paper.

- What did you accomplish?

- How will you be remembered?

- What will your children say about you?

- Would your family say you were a good person?

- Did you live a good life, worthy of remembering?

- What kind of legacy would they say you left behind?

Here's what I really want you to focus on: Are you happy with what they will say about you? Does this make you feel proud? Happy? Content? Joyful? Close your eyes and envision your eulogy, feel their words, and then journal everything that comes to mind about this process.

This exercise matters because it forces you to face the truth you've been avoiding. When you confront your own mortality on paper, you see with brutal clarity the gap between the life you're living now and the life you want to live. That gap becomes your leverage. It's supposed to hurt. If it makes you cry, good. If it makes you angry, even better. That pain is the fuel for change.

I don't care if it's painful or if it hurts. Feel it. You need to feel the consequences of what you're doing, what you're allowing, how you're living, and what you're choosing to be.

Your eulogy is not just words on a page—it's a mirror. It shows you who you've been, and it dares you to decide who you will become. **These assignments you just completed are your specific targets now.** Your eulogy is your reminder that you don't have time to waste.

YOUR ULTIMATE MISSION

You've named what you want, but now you need to lock in why it matters. Without a reason powerful enough to pull you forward, resistance will break you. This is where you find your fire. *Caution:* Before you start these exercises, warn your family that you're about to get loud and intense. Anything less, and this won't be effective.

Let's get started. Why will you stop at nothing to accomplish the targets you defined in the previous section? Answer this question right now. Say it out loud. Scream it if you're willing. *Why will you stop at nothing?*

Now let's face the harder questions:

ASSIGNMENT 7: Building your leverage.

- How will you feel in your body if you *don't* change?
- How will you feel if you let your obstacles, anxiety, depression, or hypervigilance dominate you?
- How will you feel if you let your fears keep you from healing?
- What will happen if you don't change? Where will you go?
- What will happen to you, your family, and your life if you don't heal?

Picture yourself five years from today:
You haven't changed.
You haven't done anything different.
Where will you be? Will you even be alive?
How will you feel?
You let this dominate you. You didn't do anything.

Now push it further—what about 10 years from now?
Where are your kids?
Where is your spouse?

Where do you live?
What do you look like? Do you even recognize yourself?
What thoughts do you have?

Look at the prison you've let yourself be surrounded by—
The one you could have walked out of at any moment,
but instead let control you.

How will you feel?
Feel it now.

ASSIGNMENT 8: Document your future reality if you don't change.

Write this reality down. Describe in detail everything you just visualized. The more anger and disgust you feel, the better. This will be your leverage to push through any challenge you face moving forward. I did this in Florida in a room full of thousands of screaming people. I felt incredible remorse and anger for where I was headed in my life and what I was allowing, but the exercise gave me an incredible resolve to change.

If you feel angry, good.
If you feel pissed off or frustrated, good.
It's time to harness that anger.

FORGING YOUR ULTIMATE DESIRE

Now that you can see what you truly want to avoid and what the consequences of your actions will be, ask yourself this:

How badly do you want the change? How badly do you want to avoid this future? This future is coming for you, your kids, your spouse, and your family if you fail to take sufficient action. So go back to the outcome that you wrote down in Chapter 1 and the assignments you have completed in this chapter and feel the disgust and anger that you have allowed this to happen. *You* have created this.

Feel it in every cell of your body. How badly do you want to avoid this?

ASSIGNMENT 9: Here's where the magic happens.

Close your eyes now and ask yourself these questions:

- How badly do you want your own freedom?
- How badly do you want this relief?
- How far will you go?
- Who are you willing to talk to and listen to?
- Is there anything you aren't willing to do to save your family from this reality?

Now, visualize your healed self. See the vision of your ideal life.

See your family—spouse, kids, parents, siblings—
happy because of your healing.

See your career and your business success.
How will your entire life change if you heal forever?

Now compare the two visions. How badly do you want this version of your reality instead? We're going to funnel this raw power, desire and energy you just created for your ideal future into a power source that you can access at will.

Imagine this power, desire, and focus that you just experienced is a cube that you can hold in your hand.

What does it look like?
What color is it?
What does it feel like?

Close your eyes and imagine holding that power in your hands. Feel its weight, its heat, its energy.

Next to you is a box. It might be a chest or a container. What does it look like? What color is it? This container is where your desire will stay. You can access it at any time and have it with you wherever you go.

When you need your desire—when you feel stuck, afraid, or beaten—you can open the container, reach inside, and unleash that raw, unstoppable power again. Practice doing that now. Access it, pull it out, and feel that energy. Then return it to the box. You can come back to it whenever you want.

What you have just manifested is essential for our journey. Use this raw desire when you feel afraid, stuck, or when you don't know what to do. But for the next week, practice accessing your desire and power at least once a day. Remember your vision. Remember the future you're heading toward.

Use and embody this power source and let's proceed.

UNBREAKABLE COMMITMENT

Your desire is now a weapon that you can use. I need you to do this next assignment standing. It's time to declare your commitment.

You will never come back to where you are now. During this initial process, your decision to commit is crucial—declaring where you will be and where you will no longer remain.

ASSIGNMENT 10: The Warrior's Oath.

Your desire is now your weapon. But a weapon is useless without the warrior's will to wield it. This is the moment you draw the line in the sand. From this point on, there is no turning back.

Stand up. Plant your feet. Put your hand on your chest or lift it above your head. Breathe deeply. This is not just an exercise—this is your oath. Speak these words out loud, drawing on the power of your desire:

- "I will no longer accept the life I've been living."
- "I commit to destroying my PTSD and every chain it has placed around me."
- "I will fight for myself, my family, and my future."
- "I will not retreat, I will not surrender, and I will not quit."
- "I am becoming the warrior I was born to be."

Now specifically declare:

- What you are changing.
- Who you are fighting for.
- Why you will not let anything stop you.
- Who you will become at the end of this process.

Say it out loud. Record it on your phone. Watch it back when resistance hits. This is your Warrior's Oath—your personal contract with yourself. There is no room for maybe or possibly. There is only the certainty that you put into your body through your desires and your declarations to carry you forward. The voice in the back of your head that says you can't change or heal or that you've tried this before is now destroyed.

I left Tony Robbins' *Date With Destiny* event with such intensity and resolve that I knew my success was a foregone conclusion. I would heal and never be the same person again. I truly was unstoppable. I didn't know how, but I knew that I would ultimately succeed. And I have. I have healed and I am free. This intensity, power, and resolve is what you need now.

At this very moment, decide with absolute certainty. Many of us have no idea how to actually decide anything. Every day, you make decisions with no real intention of following through. This is not a decision. Win or win, success or success. Failure is not an option. The certainty and desire that you've manifested will carry you forward, but you will not succeed without an unbreakable commitment. So once again, at this moment, stand and shout your commitment. Hold your desire and crush your fear.

BURN THE BOATS

Now that you've declared and committed to your outcome in a way that you may never have before, it's time to embody this commitment and cut off every possible retreat.

To make this even more certain, and your commitment even stronger, you need to *burn the boats*—cut off all retreat.

You see, when you were in war, I know for a fact that you did not contemplate, "Should we give up and go home and forget about our objectives?" The U.S. Marine Corps has never lost a war and never will. Win or win. This was how I operated, and I know you operated the same. We're going to bring that standard back now. Cut off your line of retreat. You will not turn back, you will not give up. You must burn the boats.

To make your commitment even stronger, make it public. Involve as many people as possible. The more people who know about your commitment, the better. Send the video you recorded earlier to every person you involve.

With this approach, it will be much more difficult for you to give up, because there will be a dozen other people that know about what you're working on. Cut off all possible retreat. When things get hard, you feel intense resistance and your brain longs to go back to what it was used to; you must be steadfast.

Tell at least 12 people, "If I come back before I'm totally healed, I want you to hold me accountable. Remind me of this day and show me the video that I've recorded of my commitment."

I called my immediate family together, including separate meetings with my mother and father, and gave them everything. A thorough description of my plan and the outcome that I was going to achieve no matter what. This is how you can make your commitment unbreakable.

Put your written commitment everywhere. Put it on your Battle Board, stick it on every mirror in every room of your house, including in your car. Look at it every single day. Remind yourself why you're doing this and who you're going to become. The more visuals you have, the better.

ASSIGNMENT 11: Time to lock in your public commitment.

Close your eyes. Visualize who you're becoming and how it feels. Embody that person. This will be you. This *is* you. This is the *real* you.

Using your desire to fuel you, visualize your vision each day. This is your leverage when you want to give up.

I have all of my commitments right next to my bed. When I wake up and I swing my legs onto the floor, I see my declarations. This drove me forward when I needed to be reminded of what I was fighting for: my freedom.

If you feel nervous about your public commitment, that's just fear talking—not your desire, your power, or your future self.

Yell out loud right now: "I won't quit! I will never give up! I will never surrender! I will crush embarrassment and my fears!"

Crush your fears with the power of your desire and the commitment that you have now embodied. There's no going back. Burn the boats.

TAKING COMMAND OF YOUR LIFE

Before you take the final step of preparation, you need to understand this: You are in charge. When and where you achieve your vision, declaration, and outcome is all for you to decide. These are your orders to yourself. You get to decide how long it takes for you to heal.

I will be your coach and your guide. I will teach you the techniques you will need, but you will be the only one who will make the decisions.

ASSIGNMENT 12: Your daily decisions.

Let these questions propel you to make daily decisions to choose healing:

- How long will you continue to wake up with the same pain, anxiety, fear, and restlessness that you've had for years?
- Are you willing to risk passing these burdens—fear, anger, anxiety, trauma—on to your children?

Remember to go to my resource page at *www.WarriorsAwakening.com/free-resources* and use the summary documents for this section and throughout the book. The tools I've prepared will assist you through this process.

I know that all combat veterans love missions. It's the one thing that we all had while serving. You had directives and commands that gave us focus and clarity. Nothing else mattered but the mission and those that were around us. The outcome that we had in front of us gave us a singular purpose.

Your vision of healing is now your mission. You're going to take yourself from where you are now to where you've visualized. You will destroy whatever is standing in your way. There's nothing that you're not willing to do to heal—to stop this from being inherited by your children or destroying your marriage. These are now your orders. You will see them through.

Success or success, victory or victory. Reflect on your vision and the leverage that you've created, daily. Remember the desire that you've manifested any time you need to feel that energy to push through to the next level.

Pull it out of your container. Hold it in your hand. Feel that raw power. Put that power into your body when needed. This will drive you forward. This is what you will need to live through times of doubt, fear, and difficulty.

Many of you have forgotten that power and strength that you once had. "What if we fail?" wasn't even a thought. It's time to embody that again.

CHAPTER 3

BUILDING YOUR WARRIOR'S TOOLKIT

KNOW THE BATTLEFIELD BEFORE YOU STEP ON IT

I would be remiss if I didn't give you clear expectations for what to expect in this process moving forward.

The first thing you need to know is that this won't be easy. What comes next will require immense effort and may be the hardest thing you've ever done. Combat will seem like a walk in the park compared to what you're about to go through in your own mind. Don't underestimate this enemy.

Secondly, don't judge your journey either. This path is yours and yours alone. Beating yourself up for how "long it takes" or the various triggers you may experience—even if you feel embarrassed—will only hurt you. Give yourself plenty of love and grace throughout this process. What matters to your healing is how *you* perceive things and how *you* feel today compared to yesterday. Focus on making one small shift every day. That's it.

Thirdly, don't compare yourself to anyone else. This will only lead to endless suffering. You are setting yourself up for additional stress, strain, and frustration for no reason.

Number four: expect a ton of resistance, especially in the beginning. You're going to be challenging some deep-seated beliefs and ingrained behaviors; the very way you exist will be challenged, revised, and updated. Your brain will not like this. Remember, what is known is safe and what is new is dangerous. So understand this going in: your brain will try to stop you from changing your reality.

There's a story of a plane that crashed in the middle of winter in the mountains in South America. Instead of going to explore and trying to save themselves, the survivors started to eat each other. Anyone who suggested going into the frozen mountainside was ridiculed—even though staying on the plane guaranteed death.

This is the depth of what your brain will do to keep you "safe," even if this safety is guaranteed to end in suffering and death. Those people were guaranteed to eventually starve to death. Eventually, however, several people decided to leave and found help. They decided to take that step to find true safety and freedom from their prison—that plane—which saved their lives in the end.

Understand that you will feel resistance, especially as you get further and further from what is known and "safe." Always remember the cannibal plane.

At this point you only need to expect the fear and your internal resistance. The sooner you realize that this is going to be uncomfortable, the sooner you will leave your own cannibal plane to find healing and freedom.

Take a moment now to appreciate how far you've come. You're already farther on the journey than most. You've already created your desire, manifested it, and put it into your body. You've declared where you will go and who you will be. You're ready for the fight. And make no mistake—this will be a fight.

The final expectation I want you to have is about the ups and downs of this process. You will go up, and then you will go a little bit down. You will take five steps forward, and then one step back. This is normal.

Healing is not linear. This is not a straight shot upward but a difficult journey. In my journey, the swings were brutal—huge highs and crushing lows—but I understood what was actually going on. I was fighting an enemy that was deeply entrenched. Just as Marines had to fight an entrenched enemy in the battle for Fallujah, you will have to fight your own entrenched patterns and defenses. Your brain will fight tooth and nail to preserve your "comfortable habits," because, again, these are known, and known equals safe.

If you feel overwhelmed right now, know that you will soon be equipped with the techniques that you need. You are not walking into this unarmed. I've also created a checklist for you on my resource page, *www.WarriorsAwakening.com/free-resources*. My page has more guidance and assistance on what to expect and how to conquer these initial stages, so check that out when you're ready.

YOUR BATTLE BUDDY

I'm here to give you tools and techniques to prepare you for the battle ahead—not just for now, but for years to come. The first tool you will need is your Battle Buddy. In the Marine Corps, we never went anywhere without our Battle Buddy. Annoying as it was at the time, we were never alone, especially in combat.

So this is what you're going to do next: establish your Battle Buddy. You need someone who will hold you accountable and keep you focused when things are challenging or when you want to quit. This person should not keep you tethered to your past habits or beliefs. You also do not need a cheerleader. You need a partner—someone who's going to support you and push you forward no matter what. You also don't need a hero. You don't need someone to come save you—not your therapist, not your mom, no one. You can do this for yourself. You only need to step up, decide to heal, and get the work done.

Your Battle Buddy could be your spouse, your adult child, or a close friend. What matters is that he or she is the right person for this role. A good Battle Buddy will make implementing these strategies far more effective. So find and train a good one. Your Battle Buddy will need to learn how to deploy the various tools you will learn. But rest assured, I will give you guidance on this.

When I chose my wife as my Battle Buddy, it made the journey more manageable. Many of the tools you will learn were vastly more effective with her assistance. She put her hand on my back when I was laying on the ground, struggling and in pain. She also called me on my bullshit. She would tell me when my beliefs were irrational or when I wasn't using the techniques I'd committed to. Her assistance condensed months of work into just weeks. Weeks of work into days. During this process, I never felt closer to her, and our marriage became stronger. She was the best Battle Buddy and partner that I could ever have asked for. You need someone like this—no matter who it is.

Okay, so how do you set up a Battle Buddy? The initial communication is critical and needs to be done in a specific way, so I have put together a script for you to practice with your Battle Buddy. However, a word of caution: Your Battle Buddy can either be very helpful or very harmful depending on how they implement the tools. If they allow you to avoid challenges, it will set you back. So make sure you visit *www.WarriorsAwakening.com/free-resources* for your script on how to discuss this with them.

YOUR POWER ANCHOR

The next tool is called your Power Anchor. You need to be able to embody your true power to change your state *at will*.

Your state is a summation of how you're currently feeling and thinking. Your state determines almost everything for you, including how you perceive things, respond to stimuli, and whether you will conquer or retreat.

When you are feeling powerful and determined, you can see a problem as an opportunity. However, if you have little energy and are anxious, you'll shrink and give up. Your Power Anchor will create an unrelenting source of power to help you push through fear. The good news is that you already have it—you may have just forgotten about it.

This power source is going to be a new identity for you. When I work with combat veterans, their Power Anchor commonly becomes rooted in a past victory from their military service. I want this identity to be truly unstoppable—strong, powerful, and unbeatable.

This concept of having multiple identities may be a little foreign to you now, but it's something you've done your whole life. You wear different "hats" in the various roles you play in your life—with your wife, your kids, or when you're running your business. These are all different "identities" and they each serve a different purpose.

To create your Power Anchor, I want you to think back to the most badass moment in your life—a time when you knew you would not be beaten or stopped; when you had unlimited power and drive. Who were you? How did you think? How did you talk? What were the traits that made you unstoppable?

Define everything about yourself in this badass moment. Name this identity so that you can step back into it with ease.

Next, I want you to choose something that represents this version of yourself and put it somewhere where you can see it. This could be a picture, a symbol, or anything that connects you to this version of yourself. Next, write down all the traits of this version of yourself on a picture or a piece of paper that you can hang by your symbol or on your Battle Board. This will be your "cheat sheet" for this identity.

Now, practice stepping into this identity and feeling the power of this person. This identity will give you all the power you need to push through barriers when you're feeling resistance.

I created an identity that I still use to this day, the "Motherfucking Warfighter Motherfucker." This guy will kick through doors and clear out hallways. He is unstoppable and fearless—undeterred by pain. He is my ultimate weapon and power source.

Your Power Anchor will bring your most powerful moment in life to the present whenever you need to conquer something.

So how do you "step into" this identity and use the Power Anchor?

- First, you have to call your badass identity forth using the name you gave it. For me, this sounds like: "I am the Motherfucking Warfighter Motherfucker!!"
- Then declare their traits: "I am bold! I am strong! I am undeterred!"
- Then you need to close your eyes and visualize your identity. Step into their shoes.

Don't be shy. Use your entire body. Pump your fists, flex your muscles, and get loud! Stand how your Power Anchor would stand. Breathe how he would breathe. When you declare your traits, do it violently and with absolute clarity. Visualize yourself in your identity conquering your PTSD—and doing so with power.

Then declare what you *will* do as it pertains to your situation now that you have embodied your Power Anchor. Do this at least five times a day for the next several days. You need to embody this new identity and get it into your nervous system. When you bring this identity into existence, it will literally create physiological changes throughout your brain and body. You will feel your blood flow, thoughts clarify, and muscles tense.

Create your Power Anchor. Practice calling him forth over and over until it becomes automatic when you need his power. This is how you push through resistance when fear hits. This is how you bring your most badass self into the fight.

FLIP THE SWITCH

Most people get stuck in how they feel—sad, angry, anxious, shut down—and they don't know how to change it. That ends now. I'm going to teach you how you can change your state in an instant.

There's a strategy that you can use to change your entire state—including your thoughts and emotions—in an instant. It comes from Tony Robbins and it's called The Triad. This tool requires immense repetition, training, and preparation, so be prepared to do the work.

The Triad, not surprisingly, is made up of three parts. Any state you're in, good or bad, is because of three things: your focus, your physiology, and your language.

Your focus is primarily your attention. This could either be mental attention or what you're physically looking at. What are you perceiving, or concentrating on?

The next piece of The Triad is your physiology. What are you doing with your body? How are you holding yourself? Are your muscles tense or loose? Is your head up or down? If I were to tell you to look and act like a person with depression, we would probably all come up with the same description. Now what about someone who's strong and empowered? How is the way they hold their body different?

The third part of The Triad is your language. What words are you saying? Are you telling yourself, "I'm hanging in there" or is it, "I am conquering and winning every day!" There is an obvious difference here. Shifting your triad will shift your state and how you experience literally everything.

Using this strategy, you will have the ability to change any emotional state, thought, or feeling whenever you want. This gives you the control you need over how you feel.

ASSIGNMENT 13: Time to build your triad for absolute calm and peace.

We're going to start off with an essential triad and that's the triad for peace. There are numerous techniques for feeling calm, but I want you to know how to trigger peace and calmness in yourself within a second, no matter where you are or how you feel.

To create your triad, answer these questions:

- If you were completely calm right now, what would your body feel like or be doing? Describe out loud each part of your body in detail from head to toe.
- If you were completely calm, what would you be focused on?

- What would you say to yourself or be thinking?
- How would you be standing, breathing, holding your head if you were at peace?

You can create as many triads as you want, but I want you to have, at a minimum, one for peace so that you can calm yourself down quickly by simply stepping into this triad. Whenever you feel agitated, triggered, anxious, or hypervigilant, deploy your triad until you feel calm again. Remember, you can change your state in an instant with the proper application of this strategy.

Here's a simple application to deploy the triad strategy:

Step One: Assess how you're feeling. I am feeling _____.

Step Two: Do you want to feel this way? Telling yourself that you do not want to feel this way will help you significantly.

Step Three: Why do you not want to feel this way? This will create leverage.

Step Four: How do you want to feel instead?

Step Five: Apply the triad for how you want to feel until your state changes completely.

ASSIGNMENT 14: Practice using your triad.

Now that you have created your triad for peace, it's time to take it for a test drive and strengthen your skill in deploying it at will.

First, think of something that will agitate you mildly. If you could measure your irritation on a scale of 1–10, pick something that would put you at level 2. Just enough to feel it, but nothing significant. Once you feel yourself becoming annoyed or frustrated, deploy the triad for peace. First, change your physiology, then your focus and finally your language.

Feel your state of mind changing from irritation to peace.

Then, gradually increase the artificially created agitation from level 2 to 3, then from 3 to 4 and so on. At every level, step into your feelings and sensations of complete peace using your triad.

Do this at least once a day for the next week until you can trigger your feeling of peace at will.

If you would like a cheat sheet for how to do this at an even higher level and how to organize your triads and your states, visit *www.WarriorsAwakening.com/free-resources* for my free resources. With continued repetition, this drill will become second nature. You'll own your emotions instead of letting them own you. One triad at a time, you'll learn to change your state in an instant.

WEAPONIZE YOUR WHY

The next tool in your toolbox is your 'why.' You're going to be refining and using your why over and over again throughout this process, so do not be surprised when we revisit this subject! Without a clear, strong "why this" and "why now," you're more likely to back up or quit when it gets hard.

When I first began defining my why, I initially thought it was, "I don't want to feel pain anymore." But the truth was deeper. My family was suffering because I was suffering. My children were suffering the most, and I didn't want my kids to inherit this. That was when I declared: "This ends now!"

My family was my why; now you need yours. You need something so compelling, it will pull you through anything. You need a strong enough reason to crush this, to change your ingrained bullshit habits, and motivate you to continue the fight, no matter how difficult it gets. Your why is essential, so do not cheapen, shorten, or speed through this. This will likely determine your success or failure in this entire process.

Define your why in as much detail as possible. I would recommend you do this in writing to help lock it down in reality. If you have a photo to represent it, keep it close to you or put it on your Battle Board. This will connect you back to your why when things get challenging.

You also need to create a visual of your why and include as many senses as possible. The more real it is for you, the better. For example, if you visualize yourself at peace on a beach: hear the waves, smell the salt, and feel the sand in your hands. When you revisit your why in moments of stress, you'll go through every single one of those senses in turn, so you need to be specific.

Create your "why" with all your senses. Maybe it's your best self, your ideal life, or the desire to live with your kids or spouse in joy. You can also anchor this to a specific memory as well to make it more compelling. Decide now: who or what will you be fighting for? Then remind yourself who you're fighting for every day.

Creating a sensory-rich visual of your "why" means building a mental picture so vivid that your body experiences it as if it's happening now. Close your eyes and imagine your reason with all five senses—see your kids' faces light up when you're fully present. Hear their laughter, feel the strength of their hugs, smell the dinner on the table, taste the moment of peace you've fought for. Anchor it to your vision of your best self. This works because your nervous system doesn't fully distinguish between real and vividly imagined experiences; when you relive your "why" through all your senses, your body floods with the same emotions and energy you'll need to fight through resistance.

You now have your Battle Buddy, Power Anchor, Triads, and your Why clearly defined. You're going to need all of these tools through this next part of the journey, because you're fighting an entrenched enemy that will do anything to protect itself and keep you exactly where you are. But your why—if it's strong enough—will impede that enemy every time.

ORGANIZING YOUR ARSENAL

You're now ready to begin. You have some preliminary tools that you can use to handle resistance, change your state, and keep yourself motivated and moving forward. From here, I'm going to give you simple steps and action items. No fluff, no extra explanations. What you need are strategies to heal with clear execution. And I'm going to break it down for you as simply and concretely as possible so that you can get from where you are now to your objective–which is complete and utter freedom. These tools aren't just for now, they will serve you for the rest of your life.

So trust the process. There is a very specific method to this. Even if you've been trying to heal for years and nothing has worked, that's okay. That doesn't mean you *can't* heal.

Here's the mindset shift I want you to focus on: it's called the five millimeter shift. A five millimeter shift every day will be your mindset focus from here on out. Every day will include small shifts and small gains. As you add up these small adjustments, even just five millimeters at a time, you'll be on your way to healing. I'm going to teach you how to incorporate all these tools, but understanding that you only need to go five millimeters at a time will help keep you fighting when you start to feel overwhelmed. We're not looking for perfection here, we're looking for five millimeters. That's it.

Before I adopted this strategy, I was constantly pushing myself beyond what I could cope with, always wanting perfection. Anything less was a failure. Now I know better and have adopted this far more effective strategy: five millimeters every day. Seeking perfection will burn you out, derailing and diminishing realistic and actual progress. This approach will help keep you grounded in the reality of your journey. I adopted this strategy by reciting a simple daily mantra: "Today I am better than yesterday. That is my win." Destroying PTSD is a journey with ups and downs, successes and failures. Seeking perfection is the enemy of progress. Focus on learning and growing each day—and achieving those five millimeters.

You've already created a new identity that you can step into whenever you want. Now you're going to learn how to permanently change your life by changing how you view yourself and your habits.

You cannot crush your PTSD with wishful thinking. It requires specific, deliberate, and intentional action. This is what's needed if you want to free yourself from your prison. So don't skip a single exercise or dodge practicing the techniques. If you apply the strategies with 100 percent commitment, you'll never be the same again.

When I first started this process, I couldn't focus or even think clearly. I battled everything from suicide to depression and chronic pain. But I didn't quit. I committed to this process—five millimeters at a time. And as I write this book, I'm entirely free from any symptoms and have conquered PTSD. This is what you *will* experience if you commit and complete this process.

What you're about to do with the techniques that you've learned here will change your life forever. Are you ready to fight for freedom?

PART II

DEMOLITION OF THE OLD SELF (SYMPTOM MASTERY)

CHAPTER 4

MASTERING YOUR WAR MACHINE
YOUR BODY, BRAIN, AND NERVOUS SYSTEM

YOUR COMMAND CENTER

You need to burn this into your mind: you are not broken. Internalize this. Read this again and again. *You are not broken.* Your body, your brain, and your entire nervous system are doing exactly what they have been programmed to do.

Your brain is a machine that operates the rest of your nervous system, which, in turn, controls the rest of your body and ultimately how you think, feel, think, feel and perceive the world. These all originate in your brain. Having PTSD doesn't mean you're broken—it means your machine needs to be recalibrated.

There are a few parts of the brain of which I want you to have at least a working understanding, so that you can understand how the machine works. That will explain how and why these tools can heal your PTSD quickly and effectively. When you understand the machine, you can change the machine.

When information comes in from the world around you, it first passes through a part of your brain called the thalamus, which then sends signals to your prefrontal cortex (PFC), which is your reasoning center—the part of your brain that helps you think, plan, and decide. But not everything goes through the reason center. Sometimes the information is rerouted straight to the amygdala—your threat-detection system.

The amygdala is responsible for keeping you safe and is constantly scanning for dangers and threats in your environment. If the amygdala perceives a threat, even if the threat isn't real, it reacts to your perception, not logic. That means a car backfiring, the smell of diesel, or even a crowded room can feel like incoming fire to your nervous system. In combat, those hair-trigger responses kept you alive, but back home, the same system misfires and floods your body with fear signals when there's no actual danger. It will immediately activate your flight-or-flight response: your heart rate will increase, your muscles will tense, and your breathing will become more shallow.

This is your body's way of keeping itself alive and has been honed over thousands of years of evolution. For your brain and body, survival is the number one focus. These responses can occur in a fraction of a second, beyond your conscious awareness, which is why your brain—without your permission—can bypass your reasoning center in the first place. The problem is that your amygdala remembers past threats and responds to future triggers as if they were similarly threatening, even if they are actually harmless.

When the amygdala fires, it triggers the hypothalamus. Your hypothalamus then activates your adrenal glands, which in turn flood your body with stress hormones like cortisol to get your body ready to survive: fight or run.

Meanwhile, your hippocampus is busy storing this memory—that whatever just happened, whatever triggered you, was life-threatening—speeding up your future response time to similar threats. This learned survival response temporarily shuts down your ability to think. This is important to know and understand. Your machine has decided that thinking takes too long—you need survival now.

So when you go around the corner and see a coat rack with a coat on it and you instantly jump backwards, that's what just happened. It's not weakness, it's a survival process in your brain to instantly assess danger and protect you.

If this reaction happens enough times, you're going to start to feel anxiety about going around corners. Just like in Iraq, where you learned that open fields or potholes in a road were dangerous, this learning-and-association pattern is a basic survival mechanism that your brain naturally uses. This kind of association threatens your healing.

This association creation can happen by choice as well—meaning that you can create this process and response, even unintentionally. Some veterans—simply by focusing on something that they are telling themselves is dangerous—can create fight-or-flight responses. By focusing so much on potential threats, they train their own cortices and amygdalas to keep reacting, prolonging their PTSD unnecessarily.

I used to do this myself. I would tell myself that driving by potholes in the road was "dangerous," crowds were "unsafe," and open parks with my kids left me "exposed." This triggered my nervous system to be on high alert even though in reality I was completely safe. Through these associations I taught my brain that *those* situations were now dangerous, and it kept the reaction cycle in motion for years.

So what is the key takeaway here? Your brain is not malfunctioning—it's overprotecting and overgeneralizing. Your amygdala is constantly scanning for crowds that are no longer dangerous, loud noises that are no longer gunshots, and holes in the ground that are no longer IEDs, because it hasn't been retrained. It will keep sending you into a fight-or-flight response—regardless of your environment.

The good news is that your brain can be retrained. The same system that once learned to fear can now learn that it's safe.

KNOW YOUR ENEMY'S FOOTPRINTS

Now that you understand why your brain is responding the way that it is, let's shift to what is likely the most debilitating reality for you at this stage: the symptoms you are experiencing.

First, understand this: You are not your symptoms. They are just an experience that you are having. You are not anxious. You are experiencing anxiety. You are not depressed. You are experiencing depression. Don't ever say, "I am anxious" or "my anxiety" again. Separate your symptoms from who you are. When you make a symptom your identity, you strengthen it, and it becomes very difficult to correct.

Replace "I am anxious" with "This is only something I am experiencing because of old associations in my brain." Symptoms are footprints left behind by old programming.

So let's take a look at some of the most common symptoms. We'll call these our targets.

Anxiety. Our first and most common target. Anxiety heightens your body's alert system, and left unchecked, it can escalate into a panic attack—which is far more dangerous. You can experience immense fear, lose control of your situation, and hyperventilate. You want to avoid panic attacks at all costs.

Depression. Our next target is the exact opposite of anxiety. Where anxiety makes you alert, depression sedates you. It shuts you down, and can escalate into isolation and suicidal thoughts.

Anger and irritability. Your next target is anger and irritability, which can escalate into rage. Anger and irritability can be symptoms of PTSD, but most people aren't aware of that. While normal and healthy emotions in small doses, when they become programmed responses to your environment, they become toxic. A major problem with anger for veterans is that it is used as an "emotional mask"; explosive and unpredictable anger can become a learned behavior to dominate situations and feel in control because it creates a surge of perceived power. The adrenaline rush, the raised voice, the aggressive posture— all of it forces others to back down or step aside. At that moment, anger pushes away fear, sadness, or helplessness, replacing it with physical and emotional intensity that feels strong and decisive. For many veterans, it becomes a learned shortcut: instead of sitting with the pain, learning, growing, and healing from their triggers, they reach for anger to feel powerful again. The problem is that while it feels like control in the moment, it actually drives disconnection, damages trust, and leaves you even more out of control in the long run.

Hypervigilance. This is your constant on-guard or nervous feeling that results in you feeling exposed, restless, or vulnerable. It's normal to be alert and aware of your surroundings, but if you feel constantly on patrol from unseen threats, this can escalate into paranoia.

Nightmares and insomnia. Your next target is nightmares, which often escalate into night terrors and insomnia. You regularly wake up bathed in sweat, and start to become afraid to fall asleep. This is a symptom of unprocessed trauma. Once you process your trauma, your nightmares will stop completely—without medication or alcohol.

Flashbacks. There are two forms: A "Visual/Intrusive" flashback is a memory where you suddenly see the memory or image. Alternatively, a "Full-Body/Full-Sensory" flashback is a full break in reality where you feel like you're back in the past. Both forms are your brain's way of trying to deal with unprocessed trauma.

Sudden crying spells. For some, PTSD shows up as sudden waves of grief or sadness that hit without warning. One minute you're fine, the next you're overwhelmed with tears you can't explain. These crying spells aren't weakness—they're your body releasing pressure it's been holding inside for too long.

Survivor's guilt. Extreme guilt is another heavy weight many veterans carry, often called survivor's guilt. It's the voice that asks, "Why did I make it home when they didn't?" or "Why wasn't it me instead?" This guilt can eat away at you, making it hard to feel joy or believe you deserve healing. Left unchecked, it can drive depression, shame, and even suicidal thoughts.

Dissociation is a less commonly understood or known symptom. Dissociation is the feeling that you're "floating away" from your body or watching yourself from the outside. It's your brain's emergency exit when reality feels too overwhelming to handle. In combat, that split helped you survive. But back home, it can leave you disconnected from yourself, your family, and your life.

All of these symptoms are linked to one another. They express themselves in groups or manifest individually. No matter what it is, they are all triggered by something and never happen randomly. It is *always* your brain's response to something that was perceived—even if you weren't consciously aware of it. The trigger kicks off your old survival programming and the symptoms appear. The good news is that this trigger can be adjusted and removed. Together we'll learn how to identify triggers, desensitize them, and reframe them until they lose their power.

THE REWARD SYSTEM: REWIRING THE BRAIN'S PAYOFFS

Now that you understand your nervous system as it relates to PTSD and the symptoms you're experiencing, as well as your triggers and some of the reasons behind them, you need to understand another critical piece of the PTSD puzzle: your reward system.

Like we've established, your nervous system is designed to keep you safe and will reinforce and reward anything it perceives as resulting in safety. This is how your brain gets you to do things over and over—even if it's destructive or unhealthy.

Here's the simplified explanation of a very complex process: Your reward system operates off a neurotransmitter called dopamine. This is the feel-good "drug" that every person wants. Your brain releases dopamine any time you do something "good"—and it feels amazing. When your brain perceives that you did something pleasurable or good (or even if you just avoided pain), it will dump dopamine into your bloodstream. Your brain then associates that experience with safety and reward, and will motivate you to pursue it again. Your cortex then connects the pleasurable outcome to the action. The stronger the pleasure, the stronger the connection. This then leads to repetitions of the behavior, which creates habits.

Through this process, your brain can learn really bad habits very quickly, especially if you perceive that they are keeping you safe, reducing pain, or increasing pleasure when you do them. For example, let's say you feel a wave of anxiety building in your chest and you have a drink to calm down. The alcohol numbs the anxiety for a while, so your brain marks it as a "success." Dopamine fires, and the connection between drinking and relief is reinforced. Do it a few times, and your brain learns: "I feel bad ➡ I drink ➡ I feel better." Now a destructive coping pattern is locked in. Connections are then formed, and these can lead to addictions if done regularly enough. This is how you can become addicted to almost anything. Anything destructive can be reinforced if you perceive it as helping you to control your environment or keep yourself "safe."

From now on, you're going to reclaim your reward system. We're going to use your reward system to create healthy habits—ones to help you and empower your life, not hurt you and those you love. You're going to learn to use your machine to be free, rather than enslaved and addicted.

You need to become mindful and aware of everything you do, because every action you take either reinforces your symptoms or rewires your brain for healing and freedom.

One common destructive pattern is avoidance. "I want to get away from this. It hurts and it's scary." As a result, you avoid it. This avoidance is immediately reinforced because it makes you feel safer. Now you are more likely to avoid it next time, which creates a self-reinforcing pattern. And the next time you experience something "unsafe," you'll feel an even stronger desire to avoid and escape because that has become your pattern.

But since we're here for healing, the next time you experience something you want to avoid, you're going to launch a counterattack: reinforce what promotes your healing and freedom and create empowering patterns. Whenever you do something—no matter how small—that reduces your symptoms, empowers you, or helps you grow in *any* way, immediately reinforce it: Pat yourself on the back and yell, "I AM AMAZING!"

Use this technique to rewire your reward system. From now on, you'll use your reward system to support, free, and empower yourself—not hurt you. You will create empowering patterns, and remove behaviors that enslave you and prolong your suffering.

Now you know the truth. Your symptoms aren't "you"; they're just the footprints left behind by learned and reinforced behaviors that have been rewarded by biology.

THE REALITY MATRIX

Everything you experience is based on your thoughts, emotions, and sensations, which are then given meaning by your perceptions. Your perceptions become thoughts that then create beliefs. Your beliefs then loop back to create further thoughts, emotions, and sensations. And on it goes.

This process explains why you can experience the same thing completely differently on separate occasions based on how you *choose* to perceive it each time. Your perception, therefore, could be completely manipulated or altogether incorrect. This then changes how you feel in response to it.

First we're going to focus on what you can directly control, and that's your perceptions—including your thoughts and emotions. You can control what things mean to you—and therefore your reality.

Everything I've said so far is something that you "have" and isn't what you "are." When you say "I'm angry," you're communicating to yourself that you equate to anger or that your identity is one of an angry person. You are defining yourself by what you just felt. If you want to quit smoking but you say "I'm a smoker," it will be almost impossible to quit smoking. You have defined yourself as a smoker. One of the strongest forces for a human is to stay consistent with "who they are." Why?

Because your brain craves alignment between your identity and your actions. If you believe "I'm a smoker," every attempt to quit feels like a violation of your core self, so your subconscious pulls you back to smoking to stay consistent. The same is true with PTSD—if you say "I'm broken," your mind and body will find ways to reinforce that belief no matter how badly you want to heal. On the flip side, when you shift your identity—even slightly—your actions will begin to align with that new definition. If you start telling yourself, "I'm a warrior in healing" or "I am someone who conquers challenges," your nervous system will fight to keep you consistent with that truth. Change your identity, and your actions will follow.

From now on, stop saying "I'm angry." You are simply feeling angry or experiencing anger. This simple strategy will remove this limitation from your identity and shift it to something you are only experiencing. This is how you externalize your emotions so that you see them as separate from your "self." Just like the symptoms that you experience, your thoughts and emotions are not "you." They are all products of your perception of your environment, which you can change in an instant.

Separating my feelings, thoughts, and emotions from myself was one of the hardest techniques that I had to learn. But when I did, it changed everything. Understanding my feelings, thoughts, and the symptoms I was experiencing as just "things" that happen allowed me to challenge everything. I proceeded to analyze nearly all the perceptions that were creating my experiences—and therefore my reality. Then I tackled them one at a time. This changed what I once considered a "Dangerous Environment" that created symptoms of anxiety and hypervigilance to simply a perception, not reality.

This may seem impossible because your feelings are so intense, but this is only because you've tied them to your identity. When you untie them, you'll see them lose their power. It is no exaggeration to say that if you implement this with complete dedication, it will change your life forever.

THE MACHINE'S OPERATING CODE

The strategies you've learned so far will be built on and deployed for the remainder of our time together. It's critical that you understand, internalize, and apply them. It isn't enough to only read the words—you must apply the techniques or you will receive zero benefit toward your healing and freedom.

So far in this chapter, you've learned that your brain is a machine. It runs on learned and programmed associations that act as coding. For those who experience PTSD, your machine is running on outdated code that has been constructed from past events based on your perceptions. Your perceptions have programmed your entire nervous system to respond in certain ways, which has resulted in the development of behaviors and habits based on the feedback from your reward system. Your habits result in repeated thoughts, emotions, and feelings, which then create your beliefs and ultimately your understanding of your identity—who you are. If this still feels confusing, check out the free resource page for a helpful diagram and guide.

Your reactions to your environment (positive or negative, helpful or hurtful) are not because you or your machine are broken. Far from it. Remember, it's functioning according to its programming. Your machine just needs an update, and this is easy to do when you use the right tools in the right way.

To change all of the above, you must understand what motivates you. Every perception, belief, and even your identity is driven by the impulse to meet certain needs, which is why they become quickly reinforced and embedded. I learned from Tony Robbins that every human has six basic psychological needs: a need for certainty (predictable safety and security), uncertainty (new stimulation, variety, and adventure), significance (feeling unique, important, and needed), growth (development and expansion), love/connection (feeling close and connected), and contribution (giving and supporting others). While every person values all six differently, every person has two prioritized needs.

We will study this in more depth later, but the takeaway at this stage is understanding that if your behaviors and perceptions are meeting at least one of your core needs, they are very powerful and therefore difficult to let go of.

Underneath it all are two fundamental forces: the pursuit of pleasure and the avoidance of pain.

Your machine will reinforce behaviors that meet your core needs, increase pleasure, and avoid pain. This is why it's so addictive to consume alcohol when you are a veteran experiencing PTSD. It meets your need for certainty, temporarily reducing your pain and increasing pleasure. This is then reinforced every time you drink alcohol, and over time, with enough repetition, a habit and addiction will be created. Understanding the root here—your underlying pursuit of pain relief—is the core. Ask yourself: What need is this behavior meeting?

By updating your machine's operating code using the tools in this book, you'll start to cope with symptoms in the moment, desensitize their triggers, and reframe your perception of it by assigning an empowering meaning to it. This will then eliminate the need to numb or avoid and completely change the direction of your life.

If you instead resort to the fastest remedy by numbing and avoiding, you will stay trapped. This is what happens to most veterans unless the old coding is updated and underlying needs are met in empowering or healthy ways. And hear me clearly on this: the need itself is not the problem. Every human being has emotional and security needs. The need for comfort, certainty, significance, and connection is built into you by design—it's not weakness, it's part of being human. The problem comes when you meet those needs in destructive ways. A bottle of Miller Lite, rage, or shutting down and isolating may give temporary relief, but it reinforces the prison and conditions the brain to do it again next time. Meeting those same needs through healthy strategies—building strong relationships, getting a therapist, finding purpose, creating discipline, or facing your pain head-on, turns meeting that same need into fuel for freedom. Don't shame yourself for having needs. The battle is not eliminating them; it's choosing how to meet them in ways that will lead to your permanent healing.

Download the worksheets at *www.WarriorsAwakening.com/free-resources* and put these tools to work. I'll walk you through each step to identify your destructive patterns, uncover the real needs underneath them, and then map out healthy, empowering ways to meet those needs instead. You'll find prompts to dig into your triggers, space to write your answers, and clear strategies you can return to when resistance shows up. Don't just read this and nod your head—do the work. Your freedom is within your grasp, but only if you pick up the weapons and use them.

BREAKING THE TRAUMA CYCLE

Now you need to understand that you're going to get triggered while healing—if you do it correctly. Therefore, you need to understand how to stop something called a trauma cycle. Trauma and triggers always build upon themselves. We start off feeling a small amount of anxiety when we hear a noise outside but think nothing of it. But then we feel jittery. The nervous system is doing its thing. We're starting to feel panicked and out of control, and we're not coping. Then we hear another noise outside, and start feeling hypervigilant—on high alert, which is really just cortisol and other stress hormones feeding off your previous anxiety. You start to imagine fearful things and your fight or flight kicks in. Your anxiety is now extreme, your muscles are tense, and your adrenaline is pumping. You begin to panic. This is an example of a cycle that will increase until it eventually dies down. But before it does, you may have a panic attack or a complete disruption to your day or night due to an imagined threat from unchecked early symptoms.

To stop the cycle, you have to interrupt the process before it takes control, which will give you the opportunity to regulate yourself with all the coping strategies you're learning.

The first step in stopping the trauma cycle is awareness. Always be aware of what your symptoms are by analyzing your experiences to determine where PTSD is sneaking in. Look for those footprints.

As soon as you recognize a symptom, identify it by what it really is. You could simply say to yourself "Oh, hello anxiety!" By calling it what it is, you will separate it from yourself, which will help you take control and cope with it. Remember, do *not* internalize it by telling yourself that it is "your anxiety" or that "you are triggered."

Next, you must break the pattern and shock the system. The best way to do this is to rapidly and explosively change your physical state—something that overrides the cycle. Do this by screaming out loud, jumping up forcefully, or tensing as many muscles in your body as you can. Do this until you are completely distracted from the trigger and the symptoms you are experiencing.

I call this the STOP approach. It shocks the system with a sudden change in state that stops your nervous system from producing more symptoms. You need to forcefully shift your focus away from the trigger by dramatically changing your physical state. Throw water on yourself, yell "INCOMING!," start low crawling, do random explosive burpees—don't stop until your pattern is broken and the symptoms have decreased to zero.

But what if you're in a busy place or even on a plane? Well here's a modification for you: you can still shock your nervous system in a limited space (I've even deployed similar strategies in a business meeting while seated at a table). Alternate clenching your fists as hard as you can, exhale strongly, and push your feet into the ground as hard as you can while flexing as many of your leg muscles as you possibly can until complete exhaustion and then repeat. I've even used hand strength grippers underneath a table–whatever it takes to shock the symptoms and STOP your nervous system from reacting further.

Next, start to soothe yourself. Repeat to yourself: "I am calm and safe. This is from the past," while smiling. Then visualize a calming place and, with all your senses, truly step into the space. Visualize somewhere truly calming, hear what it sounds like, smell what it smells like, and feel your surroundings with your hands. Stretch your body and take deep, cleansing breaths. When I first did this technique, I had a small container of sand, oils, and soothing beach music to help me that I would take with me. I would run my hands through the sand and place the oils on my face and chest. This promotes calm and teaches your nervous system that you are, in fact, safe.

Finally, reinforce this process. Praise and reward yourself for obliterating all the symptoms you were experiencing.

The key here is to stop the symptoms as soon as you experience them. Don't let the cycles progress—obliterate them immediately. Then cope until you have reached your ideal state. This is one of the strategies I use to end any trauma cycle at any time. Once I learned how to gain complete control over my symptoms within moments, I found hope. I wasn't broken and I finally had control. And now, so do you.

CHAPTER 5

RAPID RESPONSE TACTICS FOR PTSD

DEFUSE THE TRIGGER

This chapter is where we get tactical. This will be your deep dive into the no-bullshit strategies you will use to crush your symptoms and return to zero distress. Our initial focus will be desensitizing your triggers, which will make them less potent, easier to tolerate, and less distressing. After desensitizing the trigger, you'll reprogram your nervous system by rewriting the meaning of the trigger, so that it's empowering and works for you, not against you.

Triggers won't disappear on their own, and desensitization can be a very long process, so I recommend you start now. There are numerous ways to desensitize triggers. We are going to focus on the more popular methodologies applicable to PTSD.

Before we start, you need to know how to measure your distress so it can be easily communicated, tracked, and strategized. That's where a technique called the Systematic Unit of Distress Scale (SUDS) comes in. It quantifies your distress—whether it's guilt, fear, panic, shame, or depression—on a scale of 1 to 10. We'll discuss how to apply it in the next section, but for now this is what the SUDS looks like:

1–2: Low level of annoyance or anxiety. You are only slightly distressed.

3–4: Increasing agitation. You are now fairly upset.

5: The distress is painful. Now you're really feeling it.

6–7: You are now feeling intense pain or panic.

8–9: You're experiencing flashbacks or intense nightmares.

10: You are experiencing intense night terrors, panic attacks, or complete disconnection from reality. You are likely headed to the hospital.

Now that you can track and rate your distress, here is a high-level overview of some basic desensitization techniques. Keep in mind, these are examples of various cognitive therapy techniques that you can deploy with a trained therapist. The importance behind desensitizing triggers is that with the proper use of these strategies, the severity of the triggers you are experiencing will decrease. It doesn't normally stop them from happening (although it could), but it will make the symptoms less severe. Here are a few basic ones to consider:

1. **Talk Therapy**. In talk therapy, you discuss your trauma or what's happened to you one-on-one or in groups to process what occurred with the guidance of a therapist.

2. **Cognitive Behavioral Therapy (CBT).** CBT focuses on creating connections between thoughts, emotions, and behaviors by eliminating emotional distress and maladaptive behaviors and then replacing destructive thoughts with healthier ones.

3. **Dialectical Behavior Therapy (DBT).** DBT involves combining acceptance of painful emotions and changes through coping skills, mindfulness, and distress tolerance exercises.

4. **Eye Movement Desensitization and Reprocessing (EMDR).** EMDR focuses on changing the way traumatic memories are stored in the brain using bilateral stimulation (side-to-side eye movements) to help the brain reprocess distressing memories.

5. **Prolonged Exposure (PE).** PE will help you confront traumatic memories instead of avoiding them. Avoidance reinforces fear and anxiety, which prevents healing. PE exposes you to your fears gradually to increase your tolerance of them.

6. **Brain Stimulation Techniques**. There are numerous newer scientific modalities that involve brain stimulation through magnetic fields or small electrical pulses to heal the brain. This includes various Transcranial Magnetic Stimulation and Neurofeedback techniques to name a few.

If you want to dive more deeply into these techniques or need guidance on hiring the right therapist, go to *www.WarriorsAwakening.com/free-resources* or scan the QR code on the back of the book. I mentioned this resource earlier for a reason—it's meant to be there for whenever you're ready. If you didn't check it out at the start, now's the time. Use it. Equip yourself with the right support so you don't fight this battle alone.

All of these techniques can be effective at desensitizing and lessening symptoms, but you must understand: these strategies, while powerful, aren't cures for PTSD. They won't replace your hard work and dedication to the other strategies in this book. They are only tools. I benefited from working with a therapist for some time, but at a certain point the benefits plateaued, and I needed new strategies to complete my healing.

When you're ready, find a good professional to help you and add them to your team. Then keep going.

THE SUDS SYSTEM

One of the biggest breakthroughs in my own healing was learning how to measure what I was actually feeling instead of just drowning in it. Before that, every panic spike or wave of depression felt the same—chaotic, overwhelming, and impossible to manage. The SUDS changed that. It gave me a simple, practical way to put a number on my distress, to see it for what it was, and then respond with the right tool.

If you don't know the level of your distress, you can't deploy the right coping skills. That's why the SUDS system is your combat readiness meter. An initial application of the scale allows you to track your symptoms' severity, your progress, and which coping skill is more effective for you. I used this system to build predetermined approaches or coping strategies for every symptom and therefore level of distress that I experienced.

It's not just a number; it allows your brain to focus on one thing during times of high stress. This system allows you to easily identify and communicate your distress and then execute the planned strategy or coping mechanism instantly. To maximize the effectiveness of this strategy, involve your Battle Buddy. Explain the system to them as well as the strategy you must utilize at each level. Include cues based on your appearance so they can assess your symptoms and recommend a strategy if you aren't consciously aware that you're triggered. Now if you're overly triggered and can't process information, your Battle Buddy can instruct you on what to do after looking at the scale. Print out physical versions of the scale. Keep one in your car, on the fridge, and on the bedroom mirror. Give your Battle Buddy a copy too. Your healing journey is not something to hide—this is about saving your life, not your ego.

The SUDS system changed everything for me. I had a plan to eliminate any distress at any time—and this gave me a huge sense of relief and control.

Here are the keys to this system:

1. **Don't wait for your symptoms to get worse**. Address your symptoms as soon as you feel any level of distress. A 2 is more easily dispatched than a 7.

2. **Cope until you are at a zero**. You will cope without end until you are at a zero again.

3. **You must practice this system**. You must learn and practice the system so that you can quickly assess your own distress. Every time you're triggered, look at your scale and determine your level. You will soon tell the difference between a 2 and a 3, even if initially that may be difficult.

4. **Train your team**. Make sure you train your Battle Buddy and anyone else regularly in your home (even children) with its application as well. Use the downloadable script previously provided to you on the resource page (at *www.WarriorsAwakening.com/free-resources*) to help you have these conversations.

5. **Be disciplined**. Make the execution of this a muscle memory. No matter where you are or what symptom you are experiencing, deploy it ruthlessly.

This strategy is a powerful weapon for crushing your PTSD, and I still use it to this day. I'll ask myself, "What's my number?" and deploy immediately. This is one of the most effective tools I've developed.

If you also experience depression, you should build one scale for depressive symptoms (emotional symptoms like shame or guilt) and another scale for activating symptoms (physical symptoms such as hypervigilance and panic), as the responsive strategies are very different. We'll get to these next.

Just like in the infantry, where we had trained responses based on the kind of enemy we were faced with, you will do the same here. At 29 Palms, I drilled each response for hundreds of hours with my squad. How insane would it be to think, "Let's deploy to Afghanistan and just wing it!" How many of your brothers would have unnecessarily died due to a lack of preparation?

Here's the truth: Many of you are doing this right now—winging it in your healing. You're completely unprepared against your most dangerous enemy and this is fucking up your life, family, marriage, and business. You are sitting idle because it's "hard" or "triggering."

Fuck that.

LOW-LEVEL THREATS (1–3)

Now that you have the SUDS system, you need to assign strategies to each level of distress. As you learn about one you like, put it in your scale and continue to practice and refine how to deploy it.

We'll start with levels 1–3. Arguably, these are more important than the higher numbers because you will experience these more often. You've already learned a few techniques you can deploy at this level such as the Triad, which is perfect for low levels of distress. So if you liked that assignment, add it to your scale.

The strategies for levels 1–3 are more intellectual because you'll still have your ability to process and analyze. This will significantly decrease at higher levels of distress, so your strategies will be different then.

So what's effective here? Remember, when we are at a 1–3, we're feeling mildly anxious, angry, or guilty. Nothing intense yet. The symptoms are just a little obtrusive, which is what makes them dangerous—they are often ignored and then escalate.

Always start with an analysis: What are you dealing with? Anxiety and depressive symptoms are very different and require different approaches. Then rate your level of distress.

Our first strategy is to speak into existence how you want to feel with "commands" for your nervous system. For example: "I am calm, at peace, and safe." By speaking how you choose to feel, your distress will lower. Instruct your nervous system: "I am safe. Thank you brain for trying to protect me, but this is from the past and is no longer needed."

Gratitude is also a great strategy to squash almost any low-level distress. If you're thankful for something, how could you be anxious about it? For example, depression is normally caused by guilt or helplessness. If, instead, you're truly grateful for your circumstances and view it as an opportunity to learn, what would that do for your despair? Change your perception to one of gratitude and watch your distress melt away.

Another strategy for low numbers is analysis. Think through the situation and analyze its *actual* danger. For example: "Am I really in danger with someone behind me?" You will start to understand that there's nothing to be concerned about because you are safe, and your hypervigilance will dissipate. Put your negative thoughts on trial. "Is it actually true that I'm in danger? Is there really a sniper outside? Am I in Iraq right now or am I safe at home?" Then weigh the evidence for and against the two possible outcomes (danger vs. safety). Does your obtrusive thought/feeling make sense? If not, then dismiss it in favor of the truth you identified and declare your reality.

These intellectual strategies will likely be sufficient for lower distress levels. Pick the ones you like after trying them and put them on your scale.

MID-LEVEL THREATS (4–5)

At a SUDS level of 4–5, the analytical strategies will be far less effective due to your decrease in cognitive functioning. When dealing with triggers and PTSD, the right technique must be deployed at the right time. Just like breaching a door at 12 noon versus 2 in the morning will have significantly different results, the same applies here.

The best type of techniques to apply here are visualization strategies, which are perfect for when cognitive functioning has decreased but the trigger isn't overwhelming yet.

The first visualization strategy is highly effective for soothing yourself when you are activated or moderately triggered. It will likely develop into the most powerful tool in your arsenal. This strategy is called your Safe Space.

I mentioned a Safe Space in the previous chapter, so you can refer to that Safe Space now or create a new one. Your Safe Space is a mental space you create where you feel completely safe, at peace, and calm. For me, it was a beach. Whatever it is for you, I want you to close your eyes now and think of that place. Where is it? What does it look like? What do you smell and hear? What do you feel in this place? Write it down and describe it in great depth. Every single sense needs to be used to make this real.

You can use your Safe Space proactively if you know you're going into a stressful situation or reactively when you feel triggered and need to cope. This is your place of ultimate safety and peace. Remember, when learning to deploy your Safe Space, you must practice this many times a day over the next few weeks. So put a reminder on your Battle Board—a picture of your Safe Space, or a drawing—something that reminds you to practice the visualizations every day.

When deploying your Safe Space, try to practice this technique in the same place within your home or office every day. This will condition your mind to always feel safe here. I used to take a "kit" with me to set up my Safe Space anywhere (hotels or in my in-laws' homes). I had a banner that I could tack into the wall, a box of sand, soothing recorded music that I would always play, and a weighted therapeutic blanket.

Next, attach your Safe Space to any physical object—let's call it an anchor—which will allow you to quickly trigger your Safe Space whenever you need to. It is important to note that this will require conditioning! Pick something small that reminds you of the Safe Space. For me, it was a toy palm tree. When you're practicing your Safe Space, alternate feeling calm, visualizing your Safe Space, and then looking at your anchor. Repeat, "I am calm, I am safe," while looking at your anchor. Hear the sounds, smell the scents, feel the calm, and then focus on your anchor. Soon you will form an association between your Safe Space and your anchor. Whenever you look at your anchor, you'll feel the same calm you do when visualizing your Safe Space.

Another visualization strategy to deploy is called the Guardians. Visualize a group of people that you feel the safest around. Perhaps it's members from your platoon. Close your eyes and visualize them around you, protecting you. Nothing can harm you when your Guardians are there. Practice calling your Guardians forth and feeling their security when they surround you.

I often walked through an airport with my Guardians from my platoon surrounding me on all sides. Little did the travelers around me know, I was walking among them with the members of fourth platoon Kilo Company of the Third Battalion Fourth Marines by my side; there in my defense and willing to do battle on my behalf. I was completely safe.

I recommend you access the free resource page at *www.Warriors Awakening.com/free-resources* for additional visualization strategies, including in-depth explanations for those discussed in this chapter. Choose the visualization strategies that you like and practice them several times a day to make sure you're ready to properly deploy them in an instant. Put them on your Battle Board. Each strategy involves reconditioning your nervous system, which requires repetition to be effective. So get to work.

HIGH-LEVEL THREATS (6–7)

At a SUDS level of 6–7, the fight is escalating. Take this very seriously because, if you progress higher than this, you will be in extreme distress, which may result in hospitalization.

When you're at a 6–7, visualization strategies become much less effective. This is because your body will likely be in fight-or-flight mode, which means that you will have adrenaline in your bloodstream along with other physical changes. The strategies for this level of distress are therefore physiological.

At this stage, intellectual strategies become useless; instead, you have to do something to shock the system. The more suddenly you move, the more likely you are to break the cycle and reduce the distress to level 5 or below. From there you can step into your Safe Space and use your visualization strategies to get back to zero.

Simple approaches like going for a fast run are effective. Your attention will shift and all of your senses will activate. Then, deploy techniques that further divert your attention and focus from the trigger. For example, my therapist would tell me to identify everything in my environment that was green, then black, and then yellow. Then everything with rounded edges, then straight edges, etc. All of this will shift your focus away from the trigger which will stop the cycle. Continue to do these exercises until you return to a lower level of distress.

Another effective strategy is deep breathing. Deep breathing will calm you down because it activates the parasympathetic nervous system, which is your rest-and-digest state. This nervous system naturally counteracts your sympathetic, or fight-or-flight, state. One exercise I use extensively is called box breathing. Breathe in for five counts, hold for five counts, breathe out for five counts, and then hold again for five counts. Make sure you are expanding your belly—not your chest. All deep breathing strategies involve increasing your oxygen level and soothing your wired nervous system.

Another powerful technique is progressive muscle relaxation (PMR). Squeeze as many muscles as you can then relax them all at once. You can also do this one muscle at a time from your toes to your head. It works by directly countering the fight-or-flight response that PTSD keeps in overdrive. By tensing and then releasing muscle groups, you teach your body how to let go of stored tension, slow your heart rate, and activate the natural relaxation response. This not only reduces the physical strain of stress but also grounds you in the present moment, pulling you away from intrusive thoughts or flashbacks. Over time, PMR helps you recognize when your body is holding tension, gives you the tools to release it, lowers stress hormones, and even improves sleep and mood. That's why it's one of the most effective, battle-tested coping strategies for PTSD.

Alternative strategies involve intense position changes with as much energy as possible. Jump as high as you can while yelling and flexing your muscles. I also used to pound my chest while screaming. This is the STOP strategy you learned earlier. If done with extreme intensity, it will shock the system, stop the trauma cycle, and bring down your SUDS score.

These are all powerful techniques to lessen significant trauma responses in the 6–7 range. All you want to do is get from a 6 to a 5 and avoid a 7. Then you can use other strategies. Remember, you must cope as hard as you can to stop the cycle.

EXTREME THREATS (8–10)

Levels 8–10 are the extremes, or worst-case scenarios, regarding your symptoms. In this range, it is your last chance to reduce your distress before you have to call 911, dump medicine into your body, or go to the hospital. However, through using the strategies explained above, you should never even get to this point in the first place. It's not often that you go from a zero to an 8 in an instant. What normally happens is your distress progresses over time without your resistance or awareness.

The most intense coping strategy for this symptom range is called TIPP. TIPP stands for temperature, intense exercise, progressive muscle relaxation, and pace breathing.

Temperature. Temperature is the gold standard when it comes to distress mitigation. Few things are more effective than stepping into a freezing cold shower or dumping your head into a cold bucket of water. If you are in this range, you want the largest and coldest volume of water you can find to hit as much skin as possible. Is it 2:00 am in the middle of a Chicago winter and you have a pool? Perfect. This will shock the shit out of your system. Make sure you do this safely of course. Involving your Battle Buddy is highly recommended.

Intense exercise. For TIPP, the intense exercise must be bootcamp style—as if your drill instructor was in your face. Exert as much power and intensity as you can possibly muster. Nothing passive—sprint up and down a hill, do 30 burpees in 45 seconds, or box with maximum intensity for three minutes. You should be completely breathless when done. Have fun with this—pretend your infamous drill instructor is screaming at you.

Progressive muscle relaxation. We discussed PMR in the previous section, so you can apply it here too. I would jump as high as I could, land in a low squat, immediately flex my entire body while screaming over and over. Do this for three to five minutes, until completely exhausted.

Paced breathing. Paced breathing means deep breathing. So add your favorite deep-breathing exercises to these other strategies to calm your nervous system.

In summary, a complete physical shock to your system is required and the TIPP strategy is the perfect way to do it. After this, use the SUDS rules and don't stop coping until you're at a zero.

These strategies will not stop you from feeling triggered in the first place. That's not what they are designed for. They are designed to get you to zero distress, no matter where you are or what triggered you. You now have the tools. And remember, they require intense repetition and preparation, so make them part of your daily decisions.

ASSIGNMENT 15: Build your complete SUDS scale.

It's time to bring everything together. Take out your journal and write out your full SUDS scale from 0–10. Don't forget to check out the free resource page at *www.WarriorsAwakening.com/free-resources* for instructions and a template on how to do this effectively. For each number range, assign the coping strategies you've learned so far together. Be specific. Don't just write *deep breathing*—write *Box breathing for five minutes with your hand on your chest*. Don't just write *exercise*—write *20 burpees at full intensity*. The more precise you are, the more powerful your system will be in the heat of the moment.

Once it's written down, post your SUDS somewhere you will see it often—on your Battle Board, on your wall, in your phone, or in your truck. Train your

Battle Buddy on it so they know exactly how to help you if needed. This is not a one-and-done assignment. You will refine and strengthen your scale through repetition and practice until it becomes instinct. Make a battle plan for every level of distress, and drill it in until it's automatic—that is how you take your power back.

YOUR ULTIMATE REFRAME TOOL

Your brain is a meaning-making machine. Every sight, sound, smell, or memory you encounter is instantly tied to an associated meaning—good or bad. For veterans with PTSD, many of those associations have been wired to pain, fear, or danger. That's why a slammed door feels like incoming fire or why certain smells can send you spiraling. But remember, this can be rewired. Using these two strategies, you'll retrain your brain and change the meanings you've associated with your triggers.

STRATEGY ONE: TRIGGER FLIPPING

Step 1: Determine the Target

Start by recognizing a situation, environment, or stimulus that is causing you pain or triggering you in some way. Maybe it's fireworks, crowded spaces, or even something as subtle as a certain tone of voice from your spouse. Then ask yourself: *What meaning have I attached to this?* For example, your nervous system may have learned to equate fireworks to incoming fire, or a crowded space may equal danger due to an experience in combat.

Here's the key: the event itself, here in the United States, is neutral. It's causing you pain only because of the meaning your brain has attached to it. The first step to taking back control is to interrupt the old meaning and consciously create a new one. This process is called reframing—deliberately shifting the way you interpret the trigger so it no longer equates to danger, but instead connects to safety, strength, or empowerment.

Step 2: Flip the Meaning

But how do you do that? Let me give you one example. I used to interpret my wife's feedback as criticism—a rejection. I'd become incredibly irritated and defensive whenever she pointed something out to me. But when I started my healing journey, I stopped and asked myself: "What if her feedback is her attempt to love me and help me instead?" Then I decided to believe *that* meaning (even if I didn't feel like it!). I had flipped the meaning. After regular practice, I began to see her input as her attempt to get close to me and I felt loved. Note: This flipping takes training, so be persistent.

For your targeted trigger, ask: "What possible meaning could I give this that would be helpful?" Having trouble? Then simply flip the destructive association to its opposite. Write down a meaning that brings you closer to your goals. By flipping this meaning and reframing it, something that previously hurt you no longer will, and could instead become a source of great joy.

STRATEGY TWO: DEPLOY YOUR ASSOCIATION SCALE

This tool will become another powerful weapon in your arsenal. It's called the Association Scale. When I was traveling between Abu Dhabi and Dubai, I saw a broken-down building on the side of the highway that reminded me of a dangerous building outside my camp in Iraq. This triggered an intense reaction in me. I began to study the building and the landscape and noticed that it also reminded me of the landscape in Nevada toward Vegas, which meant nothing to me. I labeled it "Stimulus Neutral." The memory in Iraq was clearly "Stimulus Painful." When I focused longer on the building, I then noticed that it reminded me of 29 Palms, where I was stationed for years. Despite the shithole that 29 Palms was, I am quite fond of that base. I realized, depending on what I focused on when looking at this building, I could change its meaning and my reaction to it from one of pain to joy. Nothing about the building had changed—only my focus and therefore my feelings about it.

Picture a line:
[Painful] — [Neutral] — [Positive]

Here's how you build your own Association Scale:

- Write down your trigger (*e.g.*, fireworks)

- Identify the painful meaning (*e.g.*, danger)

- Find a neutral match (*e.g.*, just loud noise)

- Then assign a positive one (*e.g.*, sounds like the shooting range, which I enjoy).

For each step, write down what that meaning makes you feel in your body—tight chest, racing heart, or calm and steady breathing—and notice the shift as you move from painful to neutral to positive. The more clearly you define both the meaning *and* the physical response tied to it, the easier it will be to catch yourself in the moment and reframe your association. Over time, this scale becomes a powerful training tool for your brain; it shows your nervous system that the same event can carry completely different meanings, and that you get to choose which one sticks.

There's an example of this scale in the free resources for this book, so check it out at *www.WarriorsAwakening.com/free-resources*.

For the next several weeks, anytime your target trigger appears: First, stop the trigger using any of the strategies you have already learned, then change its meaning with either of the two strategies above. Speak it out loud and feel it in your body. Combine these two powerful strategies with your SUDs scale to crush any symptoms that arise.

CHAPTER 6

TAKING THE OFFENSIVE

RECON AND INTEL: MAPPING YOUR TRIGGERS

Up to this point, you've mastered your defensive strategies. You know how to desensitize your triggers and reduce your distress from any level to zero. Now you need to continue to refine, practice, and execute them. But these were all reactive strategies. We're shifting now to proactive strategies—an approach I call "coping ahead."

Coping ahead involves coping prior to being triggered with a series of techniques that will keep you from even becoming triggered in the first place. This involves proactive coping techniques, changes in perception, language modifications, and environment control. Your next approach will take the fight to the enemy: it's time to go on the offensive.

First, you need to prepare yourself. You need to completely understand all your triggers and symptoms.

ASSIGNMENT 16: Detail and summarize your triggers and symptoms.

Your assignment is to make a list of all of your triggers and the resulting symptoms. Write down what causes your emotional explosions, fears, flashbacks, and when you feel depressed. You need to know specifically when it occurs. This will uncover clues as to why it happens, which is essential for later.

For example, if another vehicle pulling behind you when you're driving makes you feel in danger and causes you anxiety, it is extremely important to be aware of that. After some thought, you might later understand that you feel this way because when you were in Iraq, a vehicle getting close to your Humvee meant you were in danger of being attacked. Maybe, on one particular patrol you *were* attacked. To protect yourself, your brain then made a generalization and now associates any vehicle coming too close with the danger in Iraq. You've reinforced this association by staying away from vehicles while you drive, which makes you feel safer, but the whole cycle is continuously repeating itself.

Whatever the story attached to your trigger is, uncover it.

Now you are going to build proactive coping strategies. In the driving example, you can develop strategies before getting into your vehicle to significantly reduce the likelihood of the trigger occurring.

Record all of your triggers when they occur, and note what specific symptoms they elicit in you. Get a piece of paper and create a log or download the tool at *www.WarriorsAwakening.com/free-resources* to help you. Continue tracking your triggers and symptoms for at least a week until you have a thorough log.

Now, unless you want to continue coping forever, it is time to take action and control. Remember: our goal and mission together is *not* to simply develop new coping strategies. If that were true, you wouldn't actually be any closer to healed. You would still be dealing with the same triggers for the rest of your life. Our objective is to completely rewire your nervous system so that you literally never get triggered by what used to hurt you again. Once this occurs, then we will change what was a source of distress into a source of power.

For now, however, the more you understand what happens to you, the better you can prepare to get to our ultimate objective of complete and utter freedom.

YOUR OFFENSIVE STRIKE PLAN

Now that you've detailed your triggers, symptoms, and the stories surrounding them, you're ready to start building a plan to mitigate these triggers by coping ahead. We're going to zero in on each trigger and execute techniques to make the trigger significantly less potent and less likely to occur.

There are two primary ways to do this: a more immediate strategy and a more general one. The first method is proactively coping immediately before an activity that will likely trigger you. For example, proactively coping immediately before going to a busy public space if you generally feel hypervigilant there.

To execute the immediate approach, get yourself into a calm state first. Sit down with your feet planted on the ground evenly in front of you. Then, begin to visualize your success through the entire event step by step. During this, take deep breaths from your belly. Step away from the visualization and into your Safe Space as needed if you become agitated. Return once you have calmed yourself down. Repeat this to yourself throughout: "I will do great. I am safe. I look forward to doing this." Do this for several minutes.

After five minutes, you will have successfully primed yourself to conquer this potentially challenging event. Initially, the situation you were about to enter may have produced anxiety, but by priming yourself to succeed in a calm state, the triggers become much less likely to occur. You will have protection.

The general method is performed consistently at specific times each day. Doing it within a few minutes of waking up is a good idea, even if you don't anticipate getting triggered any time soon according to your trigger map. By deploying your proactive coping strategies regularly throughout your day, you will create a much more resilient state for yourself regardless of your stressors or triggers.

When deploying this general kind of proactive coping, bring yourself into a very calm state as before. Then either start to visualize the successful accomplishment of each step of the challenging events in your day or your day in general. Here, you are focusing on creating the general foundation of peace and calm for yourself and your day. Once you have established your calm state while visiting your Safe Space as needed, repeat, "I am safe, I look forward to conquering this day, I have nothing to fear." Declare how your experiences and your day will be.

If you experience any symptoms, don't worry. Return to your Safe Space, reassure yourself that you are safe and calm, then return to your visualizations until completed. Keep doing this for as long as necessary. I trained my kids to do this on the way to school together as a family every day. We would visualize and recite that our days would be great every day, and then declare how we would make them great. We created powerful perceptions of our desired outcomes. Over the years, I started to see a huge correlation between coping ahead and positive outcomes. Proper planning leads to powerful outcomes.

THE WARRIOR'S BODY

This section is about three primary things: your body, your mind, and the connection between the two. I can't emphasize enough how important a healthy body and mind is to healing. With a healthy body and mind, your stress will be significantly reduced, your ability to handle distress will increase, you will have more energy and you will experience a more vibrant, positive life.

The first component is the importance of what you are putting into your body. If you feed yourself poisons, your body and mind will suffer. The first step to true health is to stop poisoning yourself.

Sugars, caffeine, alcohol, processed foods, and the other toxins that most of us regularly consume need to be stopped immediately to the best of your ability. They damage your physical body and poison your gut, which then damages your mental health.

Remove all the toxins from your system. Try a detox or cleanse. The first cleanse I did was in Fiji with the Tony Robbins Program, it resulted in me losing 35 pounds. I looked and felt better than I ever had before. Focus on only consuming whole foods and organic products and drinking plenty of water.

The next priority is your sleep. Sleep is vitally important when healing from PTSD. Your mind cleanses, reorganizes, and processes trauma at night. So getting consistent, high-quality rest is critical. I would aim for at least seven hours of rest every single night. Make sure to sleep in the same location at the same time every night. This will condition your body for winding down and resting when you are there.

For those of you who have nightmares, make sure you also proactively cope before your sleep time. Lie down in a calm state after releasing as much tension as possible with yoga, calming music, and essential oils. Once you lie down, visit your Safe Space while repeating "I look forward to a pleasant rest." I've used this strategy to stop not only my nightmares, but those of my children as well.

The third component is your daily physical exercise. You cannot skip this, especially when you are healing from PTSD. Consistent exercise destroys stress, anxiety, depressive symptoms, and fear. It will increase your resilience to distress and is crucial for reducing your symptoms. Make this a part of who you are every day—no matter how small. Doing just 10 pushups every day is better than not doing 20.

A fourth component is to express your gratitude. Journaling and regularly reflecting on what you appreciate and are grateful for is incredibly effective for reducing anxiety and depression.

These are likely all things you already know, but applying them to your PTSD might be foreign to you. These foundational strategies for coping will improve your mental health, help you resist triggers, and increase your positive emotional state.

So don't wait. Pick the strategies that you like, and begin.

ENGINEERING A HEALING ENVIRONMENT

Another essential strategy is to change your environment into a powerful ally for your healing. There are two primary areas to prepare. The first is your home and workplace in general. The second centers on the specific areas where the triggers occur. Focus on making each more soothing and less triggering.

A basic rule here: don't fight your environment. If your environment is overly stimulating and this results in you having to regularly cope— then change it. Make it work for you. This will reduce the number of triggers in your day. This is different from avoiding because avoidance is hiding from your triggers, and it only makes your symptoms worse by prolonging them.

Making your environment a tool for success is different. You can apply these same techniques anywhere you go, like hotel rooms or even more short-term locations like work conference rooms.

Make your environment more soothing. Add things that calm your nervous system: posters or pictures of places you love, candles, plants, the sound of running water, or music that grounds you. You can also place reminders of your Safe Space where you can see them daily—maybe your Battle Board can go here too. Just as important is to remove anything that ramps up stress, anxiety, or fear. For example, if a cluttered desk makes you feel overwhelmed, organize it. If calendars covered in overdue tasks spike your anxiety, replace them with a clean, simple planner. Take down negative reminders like unpaid bills left in plain sight, work emails open on your computer all night, or even photos or objects tied to painful memories. The goal is simple: fill your space with cues of safety and peace, and strip away the triggers that keep your nervous system on edge.

Next, put your Anchors where you can see them. Add phrases and statements that will help you cope effectively or reduce the likelihood of the trigger occurring altogether. Reminders of your coping strategies and your SUDS are also highly effective. Add all of these to your Battle Board and put it somewhere visible.

When I turned my office into a sanctuary, I converted it from a liability into a resource. I had my calming oils there, metal hand grippers to squeeze, and even a container of beach sand that I could run my hand through when I was visualizing my Safe Space. I also had a small, portable coping kit with me in a small shoulder bag wherever I went in the beginning. No matter where I was, I was prepared with my tools, which included anything from small smooth stones in my pocket to my small plastic palm trees (my Anchors). This also gave me the confidence that no matter what happened, I was ready to cope. Some of my tools were used reactively while others were used proactively.

If you feel uncomfortable regarding any of these strategies, this is a great opportunity to push through resistance. Check out the free resource page at *www.WarriorsAwakening.com/free-resources* for a checklist on converting your environment into a powerful weapon for healing.

LANGUAGE DISCIPLINE: KILLING VERBAL POISON

The next tool is language discipline—a tool we touched on earlier when discussing the Triad.

Any state you are experiencing is due to your physiology, your language, and your focus. If you need a recap on the Triad, refer back to Chapter 3. We're now going to go deeper into the language component.

Your brain is always listening, taking in, and processing information. It also uses what you say as a lens to interpret your environment. Therefore, what you say or think can either help you feel good or make you feel like shit. Your entire experience can change based on what you say because your brain doesn't know the difference between something you truly believe and something you say trivially.

Step 1: So just like your physical health, Step 1 is to stop feeding yourself verbal poison. Fix your language. I use that word "poison" very intentionally because when you tell yourself "This is too hard," you are ingesting mental poison that will tell your whole body to feel worse. If you say: "This is killing me" or, even worse, "This is just who I am," you are training yourself to feel worse. You are literally creating your own anxiety with your words and training your brain and body to feel defeated.

Step 2: Use your language as a tool to empower you instead. Change "This is too hard" to "This is an opportunity to win," or even better, "I'm excited for this opportunity to win because I always win. This is who I am!" How would this change your experience? Would you start to enjoy what originally caused you anxiety?

I often used to say, "I'm fucked up." This made me internalize my symptoms and identify as a victim and a "broken veteran." This phrase alone substantially delayed my healing. Just by shifting my language, I was able to initiate tangible change.

Step 3: Start to track your development and progress with your verbal communication. How has it changed over time? How have your changes and progress affected your daily mood and emotions? To track this, add a section to your journal that focuses solely on your language. Write down the good things you said or could have said as well as your negative language you used. Write down not only how you will reduce the occurrence of the negative language (for example noticing and correcting it immediately), but also how you could have changed that statement into something more empowering. For example, "I'm a failure" can be changed to "I tried and that's a win."

This will help you learn to use your language to empower yourself and stop letting it delay your healing. When I started describing my experience with PTSD as a gift from God, it was no longer a source of suffering but a lifelong mission. This shift alone helped to change a trigger to a source of empowerment. It created the opportunity for me to host powerful events, workshops, and the programs I now offer. So stop poisoning yourself. Use your language to challenge, grow, and empower yourself instead.

THE POWER OF PERCEPTION

The final tool for your proactive coping toolbox is the power of controlling your perception. We've already talked about how your perception is the determining factor of your reality. A powerful way to change your perception is by changing your focus. You can proactively cope by deciding in advance how something will feel or how you will experience it. If you were to decide to experience something positively before it occurred, this would change its impact. Changing "nerve wracking" to "exciting" will shift an experience from being anxiety-producing to invigorating, and therefore change your perception of it.

With enough practice and repetition, you will reprogram the coding of your brain. Over time, your nervous system will learn to respond with calm instead of fear, which will produce the real long-term results you need. But remember, in order to change your machine and the results that it produces, you will need to practice consistently.

Another way to change your perception is by simply adding gratitude and appreciation to the experience. Being thankful will destroy distress. Gratitude is the opposite of anxiety; they cannot exist at the same time. By feeling gratitude, your perception of any situation will change.

Keep your gratitude strategies simple. Deploy a gratitude section in your journal. This is simple to execute and will create an internalization of your appreciation.

One of my worst triggers when I got home from Iraq was the sound of the washing machine. As soon as it made a noise, I would jump out of my seat and start to envision someone knocking a window in or firing an AK-47 from across the street. For years, it sent me straight back into combat. But through the gratitude and journaling exercises, as well as the conditioning strategies in this book, I reframed it: that sound no longer meant danger—it became the sound of my ability to provide for my family. That shift didn't happen overnight, but with practice, it freed me.

You can do the same. Pair your trigger with gratitude. When a sound, smell, or memory hits, pause. Just hold the automatic response for a moment. Then focus immediately on gratitude: "I am so glad _____ just happened! What a wonderful opportunity to be grateful (or to grow or succeed or something else that you identify with)!" Then say or write down one thing related to the trigger that you're thankful for at that moment. Finally, reflect on it with your eyes closed and feel the gratitude and beauty of the situation. For more help, I've built a step-by-step journaling guide with prompts at *www.WarriorsAwakening.com/free-resources*. Add it to your journaling practice to rewrite your story and reclaim your power.

PART III

BATTLE TACTICS (DEPLOYING STRATEGIES)

CHAPTER 7

FORGING THE UNBREAKABLE

WHY YOUR IDENTITY DECIDES YOUR FATE

You're ready. You have all the tools you need to handle whatever triggers come your way. You're now ready to completely change who you are forever. You will need to reshape your beliefs into ones that propel you forward and your characteristics into ones that serve you.

Changing who you are at your core—intentionally and deliberately—is crucial. To do this, we are going to reshape your identity. When I first understood how I was identifying myself and how to change this, everything shifted. I had identified with my symptoms (the "Wounded Veteran") and then reinforced this to serve all of my needs. I was also told repeatedly "this is just the way things are now." And I believed it.

How much hope do you think I felt believing that I was stuck this way forever? None. Some of you may be feeling that same weight now, and it is doing immense damage to you. As long as you identify with your trauma, you will never get out of the endless cycle of symptoms and coping. This is the hard truth. But it's also key for your freedom.

You don't get what you want. You get what you are.

One problem is that we're taught to glorify our suffering in Service. After all, we're taught that pain is enjoyed by the "real warriors." In boot camp, in combat, and even in the barracks, we were conditioned to push through exhaustion, laugh at misery, and wear our scars like proof of honor. And in war, that mentality kept us alive. But here's the trap: when you carry that same mindset home, you begin to see suffering as your identity. Pain becomes familiar. Struggle becomes who you are. You start believing that if you're not hurting, you're not a real warrior anymore.

This is dangerous because it locks you into the very thing you're trying to escape. Instead of healing, you are glorifying the misery as if it's a badge you can never take off. But real strength isn't about how much you can suffer—it's about how much you can rise. Healing doesn't erase your identity as a warrior; it transforms it. A true warrior isn't defined by pain, but by the courage to step beyond it. When you finally reject the lie that suffering is your identity, you open the door to something greater: freedom. And that's a fight worth winning.

Your first step is to analyze yourself honestly—not just in terms of symptoms, but in terms of "who you are" at your very core. Ask yourself: how do I define myself when the uniform is off? What did I value most from my time in service—courage, leadership, intensity, brotherhood? And what have I carried home with me?

For many veterans, combat created an identity of power, authority, and relentless purpose. Then suddenly, you're back in civilian life where the battles are small, the pace is slow, and the world doesn't see you as the warrior you were. It's anticlimactic. That drop can feel like falling off a cliff and can leave you clinging to the intensity of combat, or even to PTSD itself, because at least it feels familiar—at least it feels like part of who you are. When pain or trauma becomes the anchor of your identity, you're caught in the trap.

So you need to ask yourself honestly—am I defining myself by my service, by my pain, or by something greater? Your answer will reveal whether you're truly ready to step into a new identity that isn't chained to trauma.

Now that you've faced reality, you're ready to rid yourself of the mental poison of your victim identity and everything that ties you to it. It's time to reshape yourself. It's time to be the badass motherfucker you always were—the person you may have just forgotten.

It's time to create the identity that empowers you along with the traits, rules for your life, and feelings that will drive you forward. I had to fight through a number of unhealthy identities, core traits, and behaviors that I was identifying with along with my needs and rules. Imagine every part of your being driving you forward. Imagine joy and purpose replacing tension and anxiety. It all starts with changing your identity. For further explanations on this, please go to my free resource page at *www.WarriorsAwakening.com/free-resources*.

A reminder on the repetition: You'll notice that many of these assignments feel similar. That's intentional. As stated in the beginning, repetition is the mother of all mastery. You don't become prepared for combat with your unit by firing your weapon once or running one drill—you repeat the basics until they are automatic. The same is true here. Each exercise builds on the last, layering your nervous system with clarity, power, and conditioning until your new identity is unshakable.

RECON ON THE SELF: MAPPING YOUR CURRENT IDENTITY

Before you reshape your identity, you have to understand your current identity. You need to know your terrain.

To take stock of who you are now, start with this exercise:

Write down three to five labels that describe who you believe you are today—for example, *Broken Veteran, Protector, Survivor*. Then rate each one on a scale of 1–10 for how strongly you feel that label defines you. For each label, write a short sentence that explains why you gave it that score. For example: *"Broken Veteran—8/10. I feel this way because I believe others see me as damaged and I've started to believe it myself."*

Next, add one word that describes how this label makes you feel (*trapped, proud, disconnected*), and one way it shapes your behavior (*isolate at work, avoid asking for help, overcompensate with anger*). Through this exercise, you'll uncover whether your current identity is moving you closer to freedom or keeping you stuck.

ASSIGNMENT 17: Writing out your values and needs.

For your next assignment, get out a sheet of paper and write down your values and needs as detailed below. You can also download the worksheet on my free resource page at *www.WarriorsAwakening.com/free-resources*.

First, your values. Your values are the beliefs and principles that are important to you. They shape your decisions and give you direction in life. However, most people's values have been given to them by someone else a long time ago—often by their parents or their culture.

List 10–15 defining values you live by right now. Rate each as "Very Important" "Somewhat Important" or "Not Very Important" and why. From the "Very Important" group, choose your top five. Then write down how each value shows up or influences your daily behavior. For example, if one of your values is *family*, ask yourself: *How does this value influence the choices I make?* Maybe it drives you to spend time at home instead of going out, or maybe it makes you avoid certain jobs that keep you away for too long. If one of your values is *discipline*, maybe you push yourself to wake up early, train hard, and stick to routines even when you don't feel like it. If your value is *freedom*, maybe you resist authority at work or find it hard to commit to a schedule.

The key here is to connect the abstract value to a concrete action or pattern of behavior. This is how you'll see whether your current values are empowering your healing—or quietly holding you back.

Next comes your needs. Every human decision—whether conscious or unconscious—is driven by the desire to meet one or more needs. Think about it: why do you reach for food, a drink, or your phone? Why do you argue, avoid, or chase recognition? It's not random—you're trying to meet a need. Sometimes you do it in healthy ways, sometimes in destructive ways, but the need itself is always the driver. That's why understanding your needs is important: they are behind almost everything you do.

Like we discussed in Chapter 2, all human beings have six basic needs:

- **Certainty:** the need for security and comfort.
- **Uncertainty:** the need for change and stimulation.
- **Significance:** the need to feel important, recognized, and unique.
- **Love and Connection:** the need for closeness and belonging.
- **Growth:** the need for continual learning and improvement.
- **Contribution:** the need to give and make an impact.

Understanding which of the six needs drive your decisions most often is essential. Rate each need on a scale of 1–10 to determine your top two core drivers.

To rank your needs, ask yourself questions like:

- How important is it for you to feel in control of your life?
- Do you crave excitement or spontaneity in life?
- How do you value recognition, respect, and influencing others?
- Do you prioritize or value having close and meaningful relationships?
- Do you feel the need to constantly improve yourself?
- Do you find deep fulfillment in helping or mentoring others?

Your top two needs are the major drivers of your behavior. Ask yourself: how am I currently meeting this need? And when I can't meet this need, what am I doing instead? Is this helping or hurting my ability to reach my goals?

Now that you've mapped your current self, it's time to use it to create your future self.

THE BLUEPRINT FOR YOUR FUTURE SELF

I like to call this next step the blueprint for your future self. Who do you need to be? What would push you toward your vision, objectives, goals, and ideal life?

You need to identify the traits, values, and needs that your future self *needs* to have before you can embody them. For this exercise, answer these questions as if you were advising a fellow warrior fighting the same fight and wanting what you want. What would you tell them? To reach their goal of [insert your goal]:

Who would he identify himself as? Meaning, what core identity would be most helpful to reach his goal?

1. What needs would he prioritize?

2. What values would drive him?

3. What would he absolutely not tolerate?

Now make him real. Write down the exact traits and characteristics of this future self as you answer the following:

1. What does he do every day?

2. How does he think?

3. What emotions does he feel in hard moments?

4. How does he interpret adversity?

Write this down and define him. This is your blueprint for your future self.

YOUR POWER VIRTUES

Power Virtues are not preferences. These are the foundational traits of your identity. Unlike basic values ("Community service is important to me"), a Power Virtue is a single word anchor for your power. Examples are:

- Strength: *I don't break. I push back harder.*

- Courage: *Fear might show up. I act anyway.*

- Resilience: *I endure and rise above.*

Power Virtues are something I learned in the Tony Robbins program. A Power Virtue is a top-core trait that makes up your new identity. For example, my Power Virtues for my Motherfucking Warfighter identity were strength, resilience, and determination. Whenever I put on the role of the war fighter, these traits were my foundation.

Choose two to four Power Virtues for your new identity. Don't overthink it. Pick the ones you need to make yourself unstoppable and crush PTSD forever. Don't worry if you don't "feel it." That will come.

These two to four words will serve as commands to your nervous system and daily reminders of how you will operate, no matter what. Examples include: Strength, Discipline, Courage, Resilience, Focus, Leadership.

Unlike descriptive traits (what you notice about yourself), these are prescriptive orders. When you declare, "I am Discipline" or "I am Courage," you're giving your nervous system a direct command on how to perform in any situation. These virtues become your code—they are what you embody when pressure hits.

Don't worry about how you become this version of yourself yet—just know that every identity, belief, or emotion you hold can be rewritten according to your will. When you change this, you change your entire damn experience of reality.

Now call yourself out on your own bullshit. Ask: *"Why the hell haven't I become him yet?"* Be honest about the comfortable place in which you're stuck, and about the ways trauma may have tricked you into feeling "special" (or rather meeting your need for significance) because of your suffering. Sometimes PTSD becomes part of your identity because it sets you apart, it explains your pain, it even makes you feel significant or powerful. But holding on to that false sense of significance keeps you chained to the past. Recognize it for what it is—a trap—and refuse to let your trauma define your worth any longer. Letting go of that illusion will free you to step fully into your new identity.

Now you need to give yourself leverage for this change. Instead of asking the same questions again, go back to the work you already did earlier in this book. Re-read what you wrote about what your life will look like if you don't change and what it will look like when you do. That is your "why now." Reconnect with that vision and use it as fuel—because those answers already hold the leverage you need to stay locked in.

Stop settling. Stop living in the bullshit you've been telling yourself—and the lies you've internalized—that you're "broken" and that this is "just the way things are now." Let me be clear: this is a lie. Healing is possible. Freedom is possible. Don't let anyone convince you otherwise...including yourself.

EXECUTION CEREMONY: DESTROYING THE OLD SELF

This is your line-in-the-sand moment. You're either recreating who you are into the warrior you were made to be or you're choosing to remain a slave. The choice is yours.

Your old identity has ruled your life for long enough. It was built by fear, survival, and false certainty. Your old self believed PTSD was permanent; you chose anger and numbness over healing. That may have been what you needed to survive war—but it is killing you now.

This is a false you, so it's time to bury this person for good.

Let's start by naming him so we know when he shows up. This poor, pathetic version of yourself. When I did this, I named him "the weak timid thing." I wanted to intentionally mock him. This was the weak creature that had taken control of me in the past.

Now, describe and expose him:

- What beliefs did he hold?
- What emotions did he live with?
- What rules and values guided his actions?

- How did he interpret the world?

Get honest and brutal. It's time to shine some light on this old version of yourself.

Yes, you've done exercises like this earlier in the book—but this time it's different. Before, you were building leverage and picturing the cost of staying stuck. Now, you're doing it with your *old identity* in mind. This is about calling that version of yourself out and putting him to rest. You must see the damage clearly so you never slip back into his patterns again.

Ask yourself: How much has it cost me to live this way? What has this version of me destroyed? What relationships are damaged? What opportunities have been lost? What future has this old self kept from me?

Then answer this: *If I continue to live as the [name of your pathetic self], where will I be in one year? In five years? At the end of my life?* Write this down in vivid detail. See it. Feel it. Let it ignite you to destroy this old identity once and for all.

Now you're going to sear this removal into your system. Prepare yourself for your imminent transformation.

Take the paper where you wrote your old identity's name, beliefs, and behaviors, and everything it has cost you. Now go bury it.

Literally.

Dig a hole, burn it, rip it up and flush it, or throw it into the fucking ocean.

But do not keep it. This is the funeral of your old self. While doing it, declare out loud: "This man is dead. He no longer controls me. I bury him here and now. I choose who I become next."

Now it's time to declare your new self.

You already began shaping this earlier, but this step is about locking it in with absolute clarity. Before, you were exploring possibilities. Now, you are declaring identity. This repetition is intentional, because repetition is what cements change. You don't become someone new by writing it once and moving on. You become someone new by declaring it over and over until it's burned into your nervous system.

Write it out now:

- Who are you now?
- What do you believe?
- What emotions will guide you?
- What values will define you?
- What is your new identity's name?

Like I said, I was the "Motherfucking Warfighter Motherfucker." I lived to conquer challenges and was undeterred, no matter the obstacle. You don't become someone new by hoping—you do it by deciding, declaring, and taking immediate, massive action.

You've buried the past and declared your new identity. Now honor that decision every day. This is the rebirth of who you were meant to be. Following the ritual, it's time to lock in what you just accomplished. In your journal write the answers to these five prompts:

1. What did you just bury?
2. Why did it need to die?

3. What do you feel right now?

4. What are you most proud of at this moment?

5. What is possible now that was never possible before?

Additionally, do this visualization for one minute daily for the next week:

Imagine the burial site. See yourself walking away from it, back straight, holding the desire you built in Chapter 2. Repeat to yourself: "That man is gone. I am free. I am becoming the warrior I was meant to be."

THE BIRTH OF THE TRUE WARRIOR

You've buried your old self. That pathetic version of you is dead. Now it's time to declare your new identity and anchor this new self so deep inside your nervous system that it will become who you are for the rest of your life. You are not wishing for this; you are embodying your new self now.

Step 1: Declaration Ritual

Time to speak to who you are now. Stand tall in front of a mirror. Shoulders back. Breathing deep. Look yourself in the eyes and say out loud:

"I am [your new entity name].
I am no longer a slave to my past.
I live with power, purpose, and discipline.
I do not ask for permission.
I create who I am—every damn day."

Feel it. Own it and declare it or you'll never become it.

Step 2: Anchor with a Physical Trigger

Words are just the beginning. Now it's time to get this into your body. Pick a trigger—something physical. This will become a switch that conditions the identity into your body.

Examples:

- Snap a wristband and say: "I AM [IDENTITY NAME]."

- Slam your fist into your chest and breathe like the warrior you are.

- Touch your dog tags, tattoo, or even a scar and visualize who you are now.

Whenever you feel doubt, fear, or your old self trying to pull you from the grave, use your anchor at that moment to regain control and remind yourself of who you are now.

Step 3: Build a Daily Ritual

Your new identity needs a regular ritual to encode itself into your nervous system. Your mission is to create a daily practice that reinforces this. It should include physical motion, emotion, and meaning. Here are a few examples:

- Do 10 explosive pushups while shouting the name of your new identity.

- Shadowbox for 60 seconds, throwing punches into the air as you visualize your old self collapsing and your new form rising stronger in its place.

- Take a freezing shower while repeating: "This is who I am now. I am [new Identity Name]."

It's also important to reinforce your new identity. Every time you act in accordance with this version of you in the next several weeks, praise or reward yourself with something healthy. Say, "Yes, that was what you wanted," while putting your hand on your chest, pumping your fist, etc.

Step 4: Rewire Your Environment

Your environment must reinforce your new identity. Remove anything connected to your old self. Additionally, put physical reminders everywhere, including on your Battle Board, to remind yourself of your new identity: "This is who I am now." Change your phone lock screen to your new identity declaration, write your declaration on your mirror, or put physical symbols around you. Let your environment reinforce and reflect who you are now.

Step 5: Record Daily Proof

Every night, journal the following:

- How did I live as [your new identity name] today?
- Where did the old me try to come back and how did I handle it?
- What's one thing I'll improve tomorrow?

Welcome to the new version of yourself.

THE WARRIOR'S CREED

Your transformation is not complete until you forge what I call your personal creed—non-negotiable laws that will govern your identity, your behavior, and your very life. Everything you do from now on will be in accordance with your creed.

Call this your Warrior's Creed. You are now a disciplined warrior again—no excuses. This creed will give your new identity structure and a compass in life. Here's how you will do it:

Step 1: Define What Must Happen No Matter What

What actions, habits, or disciplines must occur daily, weekly, or constantly to live in accordance with your new self? Write out at least five non-negotiable laws you will live by. Title it your Warrior's Creed.

For me, it was simple. Exercise daily. I would not sleep until this was done. When doing this, you must train your body and mind to operate this way. Do not allow the tired, weak part of your brain to whine, complain, or negotiate with you. Fuck that. When you say to yourself "I am going to go train," that's what you will do.

Step 2: Make the Laws Simple and Clear
Make your laws for your creed clear and simple. "I train every day" or "I love and lead calmly." Make them easy to remember and to implement.

Step 3: Post and Share Them
Make a physical representation of your creed and put it on your Battle Board, around your house, in your car, or in your wallet. Declare it openly to your family to cut off any retreat. This will help you dedicate yourself to your new way of life. Never negotiate with your old self. Don't ask for permission. You will always obey your code.

Step 4: Make the Creed Emotional
Tie each new law for your life to your deepest "why." Why does this truly matter to you? What are you avoiding by accomplishing this? Why must you show up for your family? Train daily? Make it so compelling that it pulls you forward.

Step 5: Reinforce Your Creed
There is no fallback. There is only the new way. Your old self is dead. The creed ensures he will stay buried. Every time you obey it, reinforce yourself just like you are doing for your new identity. Every time you break it, declare and reinforce your true self and how you will live according to your creed going forward.

Live by your creed and never negotiate with yourself again.

CHAPTER 8

REWRITING YOUR CODE

LOCK IN THE BASICS

You now have the tools to reframe any belief, viewpoint, or meaning that no longer serves you.

But here's the secret sauce: you must condition yourself to live like this. If not, your results will be short-lived; the freedom that you can enjoy and the beautiful state that you can live in will be fleeting. You will continue to cope for the rest of your life because the new meanings associated with your experiences haven't been programmed into your nervous system yet. The underlying coding still hasn't changed.

This is where most people fail. They make a shift, feel great for a day or a week... and then crash back into their old self. Why? Because they didn't condition themselves to maintain the change. They didn't put the reps in. The body—the nervous system—never made the upgrade.

Conditioning is the process of training your nervous system to adopt new beliefs, perceptions, and interpretations until they become automatic. Right now, much of your conditioning was built in moments of extreme distress—powerful, repeated experiences that immediately trained and conditioned your nervous system to experience fear and associate specific situations with danger. That's why your system can still react to an event from 10 or 20 years ago as if it happened yesterday. Time doesn't erase conditioning; only deliberate, repeated rewiring does. And this kind of cemented neural wiring doesn't go away with a single journal entry or one therapy session.

Think of associative conditioning the same way as training your muscle memory prior to a deployment. It takes what you've learned from intellectual *understanding* to physiological *encoding* so that the new association becomes your standard operating procedure.

So to change your current meanings and associations in the long-term, you need to condition yourself to embody the reframe that you outlined in the previous chapter. You need to condition yourself to adopt your new identity, Warrior's Creed, values, sources of motivation, and your new needs using a personalized conditioning plan.

The only question now is: are you ready to override your old coding? Do you want this bad enough?

AUDIT THE REFLEX

Prior to building your conditioning plan, it's essential to understand your current associations. Your associations are built on the meanings, beliefs, and automatic interpretations that have been hardwired into your nervous system. We're going to reprogram them and then condition them. Not once. Not occasionally. But every single day until they are part of who you are. I still do so to this day.

Prior to 2024, I associated the Middle East with pain, death, and fear. I knew that if I wanted complete freedom and healing, I needed to change this. In 2024, I traveled to the UAE with one purpose: to recondition my nervous system to the Middle East. I forced myself to associate it with peace and wealth. I walked the streets, saw the signs, and conditioned myself to a new meaning. I felt myself release the tension and started to tell myself a new story about the place. Now I *want* to return with my entire family. This is what intentional reprogramming looks like.

Maybe you can't go to the Middle East to reprogram yourself, but you can make a concerted effort to face your fears as often as possible. Go where it is uncomfortable to go. Face what you want to avoid. The more often you immerse yourself in the discomfort, the better. Teach yourself safety where your nervous system once saw danger. It's time to recondition your reality.

ASSIGNMENT 18: Reflex and association audit.

Write down 5–10 real triggers you've faced recently. For each one, map out the automatic emotional or behavioral reflex that fired. Example: Trigger = "Crowded grocery store." Reflex = "Hypervigilance, scanning for threats, urge to leave." Then break it down further using the worksheet on my free resource page at *www.WarriorsAwakening.com/free-resources*. Work with this process to identify the beliefs, meanings, and viewpoints you've built around safety, threats, or similar subjects connected to the symptoms you still experience.

Here is an example of how to do this:

The beliefs I have are _____.

The viewpoints I have are _____.

The meanings I've made of these viewpoints are _____.

The interpretations I have are _____.

Then ask yourself, which of these no longer serve me? Why?

You're not here to cope; you're here to reclaim control of your life.

THE MECHANICS OF CONDITIONING

Knowledge changes nothing. Read that again. You can know every therapy method, memorize every statistic, attend every class—but if you don't condition your nervous system, nothing changes. PTSD doesn't live in your intellect, it lives in your reflexes. It's burned into your nervous system through years of repetition under fire. And the only way to beat it is the exact same way it was built: through conditioning.

At its core, conditioning is this: repetition + intensity + emotion = rewiring. That's the formula. When you repeat something enough times, with enough force and emotional charge, your nervous system accepts it as truth and installs it as a reflex. That's why combat veterans hit the dirt when they hear a car backfire. It's not a thought, it's conditioning. Your brain and body learned: "loud crack = incoming fire = survival depends on moving now." That's why reasoning with yourself in the moment doesn't work—the association lives in your nervous system, not in your logic.

This is also why PTSD is so damn powerful. Traumatic events sear themselves into your circuitry with maximum intensity and maximum emotion. Life or death moments come with a flood of adrenaline, cortisol, and raw terror, and your brain brands that connection deep into your survival system. That's why you can feel like it happened yesterday, even if it's been decades. Time doesn't erase conditioning, only new conditioning does.

And here's the truth: your nervous system doesn't care whether a behavior is destructive or empowering. If you keep numbing yourself with alcohol, your brain learns: bottle = relief = do it again. If you explode in anger to feel in control, your nervous system records: rage = safety = repeat. Every time you fire those circuits, you reinforce them. That's why veterans can stay stuck for decades—it's not weakness, it's wiring.

But wiring can be changed. Conditioning can be rewritten. The same way you learned to clear a room without thinking or execute a drill under pressure, you can rewire your associations to serve you instead of destroying you. When you repeat new patterns with emotion and intensity, your nervous system adapts. It starts slowly but the changes are permanent. That's why knowledge alone is useless—it doesn't touch the reflex.

So understand this: conditioning isn't optional. It's the difference between a veteran who remains a prisoner of their old wiring, and one who breaks free forever. This is the battlefield of your nervous system—and you win it through relentless, emotion-fueled, repetition, until the new program owns you.

Knowledge doesn't win wars. Conditioning does.

YOUR TARGET LIST

By now, you've done the hard work of exposing your old wiring. You've mapped your reflexes, faced your associations, and ripped open the lies your nervous system has been running, on autopilot, for years. That was Step One. Now it's time for Step Two.

Conditioning requires clear targets. A rifleman doesn't just spray into the wind—he sights in, identifies the target, and squeezes off deliberate rounds. The same thing applies here. You must make an inventory of the exact beliefs, reflexes, and habits that need to change, and the new ones that will replace them. Without this inventory, your conditioning will be random and sloppy.

So what must be rewired? Start with your identity. Who you used to be has kept you stuck in the prison of PTSD. You've already declared who your new self is. That identity must be conditioned into you until it's automatic—until every decision, every behavior, every reaction flows from it without effort.

Next are your beliefs. The destructive lies—"I'm broken," "I'll never heal," "Anger keeps me safe," "Numbing is the only relief"—have to be rooted out and replaced with empowering truths. And don't just think about them—condition them. Train them into your nervous system until they are part of who you are at your core.

Then come your emotional responses. Rage, panic, despair—these are old responses to old neural circuits. You've already built new emotional states, Triads, and Anchors. Now they must be drilled until they fire automatically when you need them most.

Finally, your habits. The daily patterns that kept you chained—whether it's drinking, isolating, or lashing out—must be replaced by habits that fuel healing. Exercise, journaling, gratitude, Battle Buddy check-ins—whatever serves your mission must be drilled until it's second nature.

This isn't abstract. You've already done the mapping in earlier chapters. Now gather it all in one place—your conditioning inventory. Write it down. Put it on your Battle Board. This is your target list.

Don't skip this step. Everything that comes next depends on it.

YOUR CONDITIONING ARSENAL

If you skip this next step, your identity shift will fade and the impact will be minimal. But if you commit with full intensity, you will never go back.

You've been conditioned for years to believe you were broken. Now, it's time to take back control—and rewire who you are.

Remember the fundamentals of conditioning you learned earlier: repetition + intensity + emotion = rewiring. This will be the basis for the following conditioning strategies.

Conditioning Tool #1: Incantations
These are not positive affirmations. You are declaring your reality and retraining your brain.

How it works:

- Deploy your Triad principle. Use visualizations (see yourself as your new identity), physical movements with your entire body (like pounding your chest or punching the air), and the language to declare it as your reality ("I truly am...").

- Declare your new identity out loud (or whatever you are conditioning at the moment).

- Repeat it with brutal intensity—over and over.

Example:
"I AM UNSTOPPABLE."
"I AM DISCIPLINED, RELENTLESS, AND FREE."
"I AM THE MOTHERFUCKING WARFIGHTER."

Do this standing, moving, stomping, and yelling. You should lose your voice the first few times you do this. Punch the air. Beat your chest. See yourself already transformed. THIS IS WHO YOU ARE NOW.

Now repeat it. Do this for 10 to 20 minutes every single day.

Conditioning Tool #2: Visual anchors
Remind yourself of your new identity. Put representations everywhere. Create visual symbols of your new self such as:

- Pictures
- Statues
- Phone lock screens / screensaver images or quotes
- Desk placards
- Identity creed wallet-sized cards

Every time you see these, do at least five incantations. Move your body and feel your Power Virtues flow into your blood stream. Make your entire environment reflect your identity.

Conditioning Tool #3: Record and watch yourself
Film yourself declaring your new identity and virtues. Watch it daily. Let your past self remind you who you are becoming. Who you *truly are*.

Conditioning Tool #4: Reward the identity
Every time you feel strong or courageous: Anchor it. Celebrate it. Clap, shout, smile, pump your fists. Lock in the win. Remember, your brain can be trained. Reward your progress and your wins and your brain will seek it. Do *not* reward weakness, shortcutting, falling back, or succumbing to old patterns. Don't punish yourself—but only reward your new identity.

Conditioning Tool #5: Repetition across the day
- While driving? Incant.
- In the shower? Incant.
- Walking, working, lifting? Incant.

- Wake up? Shout your identity before your feet hit the floor. The moment your feet are on the ground, start pounding your chest and yelling who you truly are. Get energy into your body immediately. Your brain will love this feeling.

Bonus Tools
- Introduce yourself with your new identity (to those who support you).
- Describe this version of yourself: list your virtues daily.
- Use a conditioning tracker—see the resource section at *www.WarriorsAwakening.com/free-resources*.
- Involve your family: teach your spouse and kids this powerful tool.

This is how you achieve lasting transformation instead of temporary relief. Whether you do an immersion with me (check out *www.WarriorsAwakening.com* for more details), or you do this yourself every day for the next several weeks, experience the joy of finding freedom from what used to control you.

THE CONDITIONING CAMPAIGN PLAN

You've declared your new identity. You've rebuilt the beliefs, rewired the associations, and chosen the laws you live by. But now comes the real work: your daily battle to condition these changes into your body until it becomes who you are without hesitation or exception. And for that, you need a plan. Here's how you make one, step by step:

Step 1: Create the Conditioning Target and Conditioning Plan
Write it down clearly. You don't need to reinvent this—use the work you've already completed in earlier chapters. Start with your new identity name(s) from Chapter 7. Then list your two to four Power Virtues you created in Chapter 7. Add the three to five new beliefs you reframed above and reinforced through the Association Scale. Finally,

write down your needs and values (see Chapters 4 and 7) which will guide you moving forward. This all becomes your conditioning target.

Next, detail your specific conditioning strategies. Choose from the tools already taught in this book: incantations (Chapter 8), triads (Chapter 3), Power Anchor drills (Chapter 3), gratitude practices (Chapter 5), and identity rituals (Chapter 7). Don't just list them—be precise. For each one, write: (a) when you will do it; (b) for how long; (c) exactly what element you're conditioning (belief, emotion, identity, etc.); and (d) the result you're aiming for in that session. This will help keep it simple and practical.

Step 2: Reassess and Refine
You won't nail it perfectly on Day One. That's not the mission. What matters is that you start and keep showing up, executing with intensity. As you go, reflect on what's working and what isn't. Adapt. Adjust. Keep sharpening the blade.

Step 3: Reflect Daily
End each day with an honest debrief: "Did I live aligned with my new identity today? Where did I hesitate? What can I do better tomorrow?" This isn't about guilt—it's about accountability and course correction. Remember small, 5 millimeter adjustments each day will lead to massive transformation over time.

Step 4: Celebrate Every Win
Your nervous system needs rewards. That's how habits stick. When you live in strength, use coping strategies correctly, or push through resistance, celebrate it. Tell yourself: "I'm proud of how I showed up today." Give your brain a dopamine hit to reinforce the victory.

Step 5: Schedule Your Conditioning Time
Repetition is your new model. You don't "find" time—you create it. Schedule three non-negotiable conditioning blocks each day: morning,

midday, and evening. Keep them short but powerful—15 to 30 minutes. Use this time for your chosen strategies: incantations, identity rituals, visualization drills, or reviewing your conditioning inventory. Make these blocks untouchable.

Step 6: Anticipate and Conquer Challenges
List every logistical or emotional obstacle ahead of time. "I don't have privacy at work." "I'll be tired at night." "My schedule is packed."

Now write your countermeasures next to each one. Take walks, sit in your car, adjust your timing. Don't let comfort or fear stop you. There is no excuse you cannot combat if you plan for it. Write your Battle Plan against resistance now, so that when it shows up, you've already crushed it.

CHAPTER 9

REBUILDING THE BATTLEFIELD OF YOUR DAILY LIFE

COMMAND EVERY HOUR

Now that you've forged your new identity and rewired your nervous system, you're ready for the next objective: mastery of your daily life. This is where everything gets tested. This is a mandate.

If you don't revamp your daily routines, you'll sabotage everything you've built. You'll find yourself stuck in cycles of resistance. You'll feel like two people: the new identity you declared and the old one still running your actual behavior. That tension between your vision and your habits will ruin your progress. You'll take one step forward and one step backwards over and over again.

Your nervous system runs on patterns. It craves familiar and daily routines. If you've been numbing, avoiding, sleeping in, or isolating for months or years, you have been etching those routines into your neurology. This may actually involve unconscious conditioned tendencies. Unless you rewrite them, they'll work against your willpower, motivation, and your commitment to grow and heal into who you're becoming.

That's why this chapter is critical. Once you've rebuilt your inner world, you must then rebuild your outer world—your *actual life*—and all your daily habits and patterns. What time you wake up, how you start your day, what you say to yourself, and how you move your body (to name a few). These things *create* your results and will largely determine your outcome.

Here's the rule: If your habits don't serve your new identity, they serve your old bullshit.

You can't keep habits from the man you used to be. You can't hit snooze and expect to wake up victorious. You can't avoid journaling, avoid your family, or skip your incantations and expect to feel powerful. Just like you can't avoid eating healthily and exercising and expect to be built like Dwayne "The Rock" Johnson. You must rebuild every habit from the ground up and intentionally align it with your mission and new identity.

I used to wake up late, lie in bed, and delay facing any difficulty or challenges. This alone fed depression, anxiety, and shame. What do I do now? I explode out of bed with wild intensity, I scare people down the hall when I forget I'm no longer at home. I am filled with energy, intention, and direction. I wake up consistently before my alarm because my body *wants* to win now. It's trained like a machine. This wasn't just a mindset shift—I built this.

This chapter is about making that level of change. You're going to evaluate every piece of your day and ask:

Does this pattern empower my new identity... or does it empower my pain?

That question will guide you and help you determine what needs to be removed.

Welcome to one of the final phases of your transformation: mastery of your time and each action you take.

EXPOSE THE ENEMY IN YOUR HABITS

Before we start building new patterns, you must understand what is already in place. What habits have you created? It is again time to look in the mirror with brutal honesty, as we've done at every stage of this journey so far.

So here's your mission: Assess your habits, routines, and patterns—hour by hour, day by day. What do you do consistently? What do you say to yourself? What emotions do you default to? What actions are repeated daily? This isn't just about what you do physically. It's about thought loops, emotional reactions, numbing patterns, and rituals—good or bad.

Grab a notebook or use the worksheet in your free resource section at *www.WarriorsAwakening.com/free-resources*. Break down a full day: morning, midday, and evening. In Column 1, write down the habit or routine. In Column 2, list the *impact*, good or bad, short-term or long-term. Does it help or hurt your energy, your emotions, your focus, and your relationships? Is this really moving you toward your objective of absolute freedom?

Then comes Column 3: the gut punch. Ask yourself: *What am I getting out of this?*

Every pattern you repeat, even the destructive ones, is meeting a need. If they weren't, you wouldn't still be doing them. You must identify what that need is.

Some habits give you certainty: your morning coffee, your after-work routine. Others give you connection, like bonding over junk food with friends. Some habits are attempts at relief: stress eating, smoking, drinking alcohol, zoning out with your phone. Most destructive patterns numb pain, reduce anxiety, or bring momentary comfort.

Don't judge them. Analyze them. Even a habit like overeating might be meeting a need for comfort, control, love, stimulation, or stress relief. Understand it first, then you can change it.

This is how you reclaim yourself: by facing the truth. Once you know what a habit is giving you, or doing to you, you can replace it with something better. But without this clarity, you'll be shooting blind. You'll try to stop the behavior without understanding *why you learned it in the first place*, and that rarely works. Understand this: these habits can progress into full-blown addictions. They must be dealt with.

Do you want to stop drinking every night? You need to know whether it's for relief, escape, or connection. Different needs require different replacements.

This is also why two people might do the same thing, like smoking, but for entirely different reasons. One person might smoke to relax, while another smokes to feel connected to a group. Those are two different needs, and two different strategies are required to address them.

So look at your routines. What are they creating in your life? What do they reinforce? Do they align with your new identity or keep you anchored to your past? *Is it moving you forward?*

You don't need to understand everything perfectly. Just write what comes up with brutal honesty. This exercise is your habit audit. Do the work. Assess your habits. Face your patterns. Because next, we're going to track and rebuild them for good.

FORCING HABIT CHANGE AT ANY COST

You've assessed your habits. You've looked at what's helping you and what's holding you back. Now comes the moment which will decide your outcome in your battle against your ingrained habits. Why will this shit change—no matter what?

The key is leverage.

Anyone can change anything with sufficient leverage—no matter the addiction or history. You just need a reason powerful enough to shatter the denial and resistance. Earlier in this book, you wrote about what your life will look like in five or 10 years from now if you don't change. That work was critical—it forced you to face the long-term consequences of staying the same.

Now, we're going to stack more on top of that. This isn't about imagining the future anymore—it's about burning it into your nervous system today. You must create *pain in the present* around staying stuck, and *intense pleasure in the present* around change. Your earlier vision exercise gave you the map. This leverage work is about loading the weapon and pulling the trigger.

Remember, you are not just tweaking your life—you are destroying the parts of yourself that no longer serve you and replacing them with sources of power. This is where you build an unstoppable reason, a purpose so fierce it drives you through every ounce of resistance. Because make no mistake—your body will resist this change. Your nervous system will fight back. It will scream that change is dangerous.

That's why leverage matters. It ties your pain and your pleasure to action now—not someday. This is how you force your nervous system to obey and push past its resistance—by reminding it, over and over, that the cost of staying the same is unbearable, and the reward of change is freedom.

Here's the strategy:

Step 1: Reconnect to Your Mission

What is your outcome? What did you declare back in Chapter 1? What vision did you see for your life? Freedom from PTSD, emotional power, unending joy, or simply daily peace? Write it down again. Get clear. See it vividly and feel it in your body. Pull out your earlier declaration and rewrite it here in present tense. This isn't new work—it's reinforcement. The more often you revisit and rewrite your outcome, the more your nervous system will accept it as real.

Step 2: Identify the Changes Your Outcome Requires

Look at your current routines. What has to go? What must stay? What needs to be added to get there? Align your daily actions with your identity. This is where you connect your vision to your habits. If the new version of you demands power, peace, and purpose—then every habit must support those requirements.

Step 3: Rebuild Your Leverage

Yes, you already explored the pain of staying the same earlier in this book. This step is about drilling it in. Repetition is not redundancy—it's conditioning. Ask yourself:

- What will it cost me and my family if I don't change these habits?
- What pain will I continue to live with?
- Who else will suffer if I stay the same?

Step 4: Flip It: What Will I Gain If I Make This Change?

You've pictured your future before, but now it's time to anchor it emotionally. Feel it in your body as if it's already yours. Imagine waking up without anxiety. Connecting deeply with your spouse and kids. Living with peace and power. Write this vision in detail—not as a dream, but as a present reality. This repetition makes it stick; it's how you condition victory.

Step 5: Teach It

Imagine your child, your spouse, or your best friend asking you, "How do I get to [outcome]?" How would you tell them to live day to day? What would you say they must do? Write down your answer. That's your strategy.

Final Step: Revisit Your Battle Board

By now, your Battle Board should already be alive with the raw truth of your mission—your outcomes, your why, your identity, your leverage. Now it's time to level it up. Refine it. Strengthen it. This is where you fuse it all together. Title your board (if you didn't already) with a name that ignites you—Operation Victory, My Freedom Plan, Life on My Terms. Add images and words that capture the life you are conditioning into your nervous system—a thriving family, a strong body, peace, adventure, and unstoppable growth. Place it somewhere unmissable. Every time your eyes fall on it, your nervous system gets a fresh reminder: this is who I am now, this is where I'm going, and nothing will stop me. This isn't clutter—it's command and control. One board. One mission. Your life on your terms.

STRATEGIES FOR EMPOWERING HABITS

You've identified the habits that no longer serve you, your mission has been built and the leverage you need has been created. It is now time to attack. This section contains the strategies you will need to fully replace and install new empowering habits that will lead you to your ultimate freedom. Deploy them with consistency, focus, and repetition.

Step 1: Identify Resistance

You must first assess your opponent. What challenges or resistance will you face? Internal or external? Write them down. Maybe it's "I've done this for too long to change" or "I don't have time." That's a limiting belief—and absolute bullshit. With enough leverage and strategy, anything can change. Write down the obstacle and then the countermeasure you will deploy. How will you overcome this resistance? If you're stuck, ask yourself: *What would I tell someone else to do if they had this excuse?* This is your answer.

Step 2: Repeat Relentlessly

Habits are built through repetition. Do the new habit *every damn day*. No skipping. No excuses. Do it until it becomes automatic. The more frequently you do it, the faster it gets embedded.

Step 3: Attach Identity and Meaning

This is critical. Don't just go through the motions; become the kind of person who does it no matter what. Say it out loud. "I exercise daily because this is who I am." "I meditate because I am at peace." Say it as you do it. Over and over. This makes the habit part of who you are. Remember, one of the strongest forces for a human is the need to stay consistent with how they define themselves. Use that approach to your advantage.

Step 4: Block the Time

Put it in your calendar. Set an alarm. Once scheduled, it's non-negotiable. Period.

Step 5: Start Small to Win Big

Create momentum. Start with something so easy you *can't* fail. Want to exercise? Commit to 10 pushups. This is enough to start and will make it nearly impossible to fail. The point is to build consistency. You'll scale up fast once momentum kicks in.

Step 6: Stack It

Attach the new habit to one you already do. Drink coffee every morning? Great. Right after coffee, drop and do three push-ups. Eventually, your new habit will anchor itself.

Step 7: Reward Yourself

Celebrate each win with reinforcement. Positive emotion strengthens habit. Smile. Say, "Hell yes!" Do a victory gesture. This anchors joy and will train your brain.

Step 8: Track It

Every time you complete your new habit, mark it. Use a journal, checklist, or app. Visual tracking gives you proof that you're becoming who you say you are.

Deploy these eight strategies daily. No excuses. If one tactic fails, do something else. If that one fails, pivot again. What matters is that you don't quit.

When I rebuilt my life after years of self-sabotage, I used these exact tools. I changed everything: my food, workouts, how I spoke, and even how I thought. It all started small, but I showed up every day. And eventually, those habits rewired my brain and reshaped my future.

Now it's your turn. Open your tracker worksheet, choose your habit, and deploy the strategy.

REINFORCEMENT STRATEGIES FOR PERMANENT CHANGE

This is it. The final nail in the coffin of your old life. Everything you've done in this chapter, every habit identified, every destructive pattern exposed, every strategy deployed—they mean nothing if you don't reinforce it and commit with total intensity.

First off, reinforcement is non-negotiable. You've done versions of this before in earlier chapters—declaring your identity, celebrating wins, conditioning gratitude. But here, reinforcement takes on a different mission: locking in your new habits so they become automatic. This is where you move from practice to permanence. Reinforcement is how you signal to your brain: "This matters. Do it again. This is how we behave." Without reinforcement, even the best habits can fade.

So here's the difference this time: earlier, reinforcement was about getting you started. Here, it's about making sure your nervous system encodes your new habits for life. You already know the tools: praise yourself, use physical touch, reward small victories, share wins with people who lift you up. But now you need to apply them deliberately and intentionally after every single habit rep. No exceptions.

Build your ritual now. For example: "Every morning I train, because I am a fucking warrior." Slam your chest, jump, and shout: "I AM DISCIPLINE. I LOVE MY BODY. I AM UNSTOPPABLE!"

Or every time you choose a coping strategy over numbing, smile, hug yourself, and yell: "I LOVE WHO I'M BECOMING. PTSD HAS NO POWER OVER ME!"

That's not cheesy. That's you rewiring your nervous system with loads of dopamine.

Now write out your reinforcement plan. For every new habit, document the exact reward strategy you will deploy. Make it energizing. The brain doesn't change because you "think" about something, it changes because you feel it in your body.

Now it's time for Absolute Commitment.

You've come too far to half-ass this. Your identity, your mission, and your future demands full alignment. That means you must burn the boats. No retreat. No "maybe." First, reflect on the commitments you've made during our time together. It's time to revisit your journal and your Battle Board. Remember your "why"s and declare them out loud. Next are regular reminders of your commitment. Set alarms to yell out your commitment. Remember to create visual representations and put them *everywhere*. Throughout the day recite your Warrior's Creed or adopt a general mantra.

Furthermore, your execution must be tracked. Hold yourself accountable. If you fail, recommit immediately without self-pity. Focus on action and adjustment. The simplest way to track your execution is with a daily log. Don't overcomplicate it—use a notebook, a journal, or even a whiteboard on your wall. At the top, list your new habits and conditioning drills. Each day, mark a ✓ when you complete them and an ✘ if you don't. At the end of the week, review: where did you hit the mark? Where did you fall short? This will give you tangible proof of your progress. If you see too many ✘s, recommit immediately. Adjust your strategy if needed, but never let more than one miss go uncorrected. This system keeps you brutally honest and ensures momentum never dies.

It is up to you to decide not to live another minute of your old bullshit. It is time to change. Now. But to make this shift concrete, you have to start small. Choose *one* new habit, *one* reinforcement ritual, and *one* tracking method you will start today. Write them down in your journal or on your tracker. For example: "Habit: 15 minutes of evening reflection. Reinforcement: fist pump and victory shout after completion. Tracking: daily ✓ on my wall chart." This is not theory—this is the execution plan that locks your new identity into your nervous system. Start tonight, and tomorrow, do it again. Build momentum immediately. Once the habit is automatic—start building others in the same way.

PART IV

HOLDING THE GROUND (MAINTENANCE)

CHAPTER 10

THE SABOTEURS OF HEALING

WHAT HEALING KILLERS ARE AND WHY THEY ARE SO DANGEROUS

You've reprogrammed your identity, installed the right habits, and generated unstoppable leverage. Now we turn to the hidden threats that, if left unchecked, will destroy all the progress you've built. These are not just minor obstacles. They are killers, and make no mistake, these are the patterns that take veterans' lives every day across our great nation.

I call them the Healing Killers. These are the patterns, beliefs, behaviors, and emotional traps that will enslave you, aggravate your symptoms, and keep you stuck. There are the normal Healing Killers— and then there's an upper echelon that will really fuck you up, which I call the Ultimate Healing Killers.

If you do not destroy these patterns, you will stay trapped, without the healing and freedom you are so close to attaining. So let's bring them into the light.

1. Identifying with PTSD

"This is just who I am." Bullshit. PTSD is a conditioned response, not your identity. Identifying with your trauma will prevent healing. If you believe that PTSD is who you are, you're doomed to repeat the same cycles. The moment you believe "This is me," you've locked yourself into a lifestyle of symptoms.

2. Lone-wolf healing

Refusing help from professionals is foolish pride pretending to be strength. "I don't need anybody!" is a huge lie. Seeking assistance is critical to your success. You don't have to work with a therapist, but you do need a team. A mentor, a coach, someone who has been there and done that. You can even reach out to me. Just like in service, you can learn from those who are more experienced.

3. Coping through numbing

Porn, booze, binge-watching TV, emotional shutdown—all to mask pain. They can become incredibly addictive. This healing killer is absolute destruction disguised as relief. You may think binging Netflix, scrolling endlessly, or gaming for hours is harmless—it's not. These numbing behaviors reinforce avoidance and teach your nervous system to escape instead of confront. You're not soothing symptoms, you're sedating and enhancing them.

4. Isolation

Similar to numbing, this Healing Killer involves pulling away from those around you in the name of "safety." This commonly leads to depression. Connection is healing; isolation is damaging. There are a variety of reasons why people do this. Perhaps it's fear or you've associated being around other people as uncomfortable or triggering.

This is a highway to depression. The belief that you're "safer alone" is a lie. I used to avoid my kids because their sudden noises triggered me. That avoidance only deepened my guilt.

5. Drug use

Drugs, legal or illegal, become traps when they're used to *escape* instead of to *heal*. There's a critical difference between working with a doctor to use prescribed medication as part of your recovery, and numbing yourself to avoid facing your demons. One is treatment. The other is avoidance. Healing requires you to build strength in facing reality, not running from it. If you're using substances to check out, you're feeding the problem—not solving it.

6. Half-ass effort

There can be no change without intensity and consistency. If you dabble, you will stay stuck. Healing only comes through full commitment. There is no halfway. Half-assed effort is death to any progress. You need absolute commitment. Track your progress, set non-negotiable goals, and revisit your vision. Your healing isn't optional.

7. Believing healing is impossible

If you've already decided you can't heal, then you won't. Belief is step one. Without it, no strategy in the world can save you. If you don't believe, you won't try. And if you don't try, you won't change.

8. Avoidance

Avoiding your triggers, feelings, or symptoms avoids the battle and therefore the growth. Every time you avoid a trigger, you are more likely to avoid the trigger again. Courage isn't the absence of fear—it's taking action despite it.

9. Belief that PTSD makes you weak

If you carry shame for your symptoms, you will never heal them. PTSD is not weakness, it is simply your nervous system getting stuck in the past. Believing that PTSD makes you weak will lead you to dark places. You may judge yourself, pour toxic language into your brain for experiencing it, or even deny PTSD altogether because you're embarrassed and ashamed. This commonly leads to pervasive shame and guilt.

10. Toxic language and self-defeating beliefs

We addressed this in Chapter 6, so remember: Language shapes your reality. Toxic language will derail your healing.

11. Numbing addictions

This is far beyond coping through numbing as listed above. This refers to behavior patterns that have developed into full-blown addictions. Your brain will quickly become dependent on whatever you do to avoid and reduce pain, whether it is alcohol, gambling, or social media.

12. Survivor's guilt and shame

The final, and arguably most deadly, Healing Killer is shame and guilt for your own survival. We'll discuss this in more detail in the next section, because this one is important. For now, understand that this guilt will lead you to many other Healing Killers if you are not careful. Survivor's guilt whispers lies like, "I don't deserve to be here" or "It should've been me." Those thoughts can spiral into despair, rage, and even suicide if left unchecked. The truth is, you made it home for a reason—and burying yourself in shame dishonors both your life and the brothers you lost. They would never want your survival to be a prison. The way you honor them is by living—fully, fiercely, and with purpose. This is not about forgetting them; it's about refusing to let guilt keep you from the life they would give anything to still have.

THE FIRST ULTIMATE KILLER: NUMBING ADDICTIONS

There are two Ultimate Healing Killers: Numbing addictions and survivor's guilt. These are not like the others. The earlier Healing Killers can stall your progress or drag you backward, but these two will bury you if left unchecked. They strike deeper, attach themselves tighter, and have the power to erase everything you've fought for. That's why they demand their own focused assault.

I've already talked about just how dangerous this Healing Killer is, but here's the difference: the others will chip away at you, but numbing addictions will kill you. They hijack your nervous system, rewire your brain's reward pathways, and convince you that you're safe with them. Once that wiring is locked in, every effort to move forward gets sabotaged from the inside.

The most common numbing addiction is alcohol, where you drink yourself to sleep, calm down, go out in public, avoid your next panic attack, flashback or nightmare, or to just not feel the pain for a while. Not only will this do immense damage to your physical body, it will also destroy your career, your relationships, and your passions. You will never heal from PTSD by falling prey to this ultimate killer.

The problem with alcohol and so many other numbing addictions is that it's socially acceptable despite being such a dangerous drug. If you struggle with sexual addictions, gambling, alcoholism, rage, or any variety of other numbing addictions—including your phone— this deserves your utmost attention. Even if you're not medically considered an alcoholic, but you need to get high or drunk every day, this is an Ultimate Healing Killer.

Numbing addictions can also include adrenaline, violence, shopping, and anger. What starts out as a brief escape tool soon becomes a fully-fledged addiction at the sign of any pain. I struggled with addictions to video games, pornography, anger, and alcohol for years. I didn't understand the damage they were causing until I faced them head-on.

Depending on the severity of the addiction, you may need to seek expert assistance as well. For some, that may mean reaching out to a 12-Step group, a detox program, or even a rehab facility. None of these paths are shameful—they are lifelines, and for many warriors, they are the first real step toward freedom. The only mistake you can make now is doing nothing.

THE SECOND ULTIMATE KILLER: SURVIVOR'S SHAME AND GUILT

The next Ultimate Healing Killer is shame and guilt. Make no mistake, these bastards will fuck up your healing if you let them. They are silent executioners.

Survivor's guilt. It's the lie that says, "You lived, they didn't. You could've done more." It plays like a broken record: *What if I had reacted faster? Made a different call? Pushed harder?* This is mental storytelling. And it's pure fiction. You're trying to rewrite history by judging yourself about situations that you can't do a damn thing about now.

I lived it.

I was stationed at a forward operating base in the Al Anbar Province of Iraq. One night, I sat on a defensive position with a .50 cal aimed downrange. Across the street, Iraqi soldiers manned their post. I was their guardian angel and supporting position. A sniper opened fire. I radioed my sergeant for permission to engage. But we had no positive ID. His order was clear: *Do not fire until you see the enemy and what's behind him.* As you know, a .50 cal machine gun would tear through four or five houses in Iraq before stopping.

So I sat there. Watched. Heard the shots. One by one, those soldiers were taken out.

For years, I carried intense guilt like a body on my shoulders. *What if I had done more? Could I have saved them? Did I fail them? What if I looked harder and had gotten that PID?*

I had so many nightmares about the gunshots that I heard and the people that were killed. They died. I lived. I was responsible... or so I felt.

Here's the truth you need to hear: guilt is a normal, human response. It proves you have a conscience, that you care about life, that you carry integrity in your soul. Without guilt, we'd be something far less than human. But combat is not a normal human experience. It forces your mind to fit human emotions into inhuman circumstances. That's why guilt after combat can feel unbearable—because you're trying to apply normal human conscience to a battlefield where nothing was normal, nothing was fair, and nothing was fully in your control.

Here's the truth: I followed my orders. I acted with integrity. I made the best decision I could under fire. The orders of the sergeant made sense. Therefore, this guilt wasn't rooted in reality: it was rooted in endlessly replaying a battle I could never win.

Shame is even deadlier. Guilt says you did something wrong. Shame says *you are* something wrong. Maybe you feel weak for having PTSD. Maybe you feel broken because others seem "fine." Maybe you're hiding symptoms, pretending everything's okay because you're ashamed of being triggered or revealing this "weakness" you believe you have.

And here's the truth you need to face: shame often runs deeper than combat. Ask yourself—did you always feel weak, unworthy, or broken in some way, even before you deployed? Did those beliefs live in the background of your life, only to be lit on fire by combat? That's how shame works. It's about who we believe we are at our core. Combat may have aggravated something already there, making it feel permanent and inescapable.

Destroying guilt and shame does not dishonor the fallen—it honors them. They did not sacrifice so you could suffer without end. They would want you to live, to thrive, to find joy again. The greatest way to honor their memory is not with endless pain, but by restoring your strength, reclaiming your happiness, and living fully free. You honor your brothers not by breaking down, but by *rising up* and *kicking ass* in their name.

Is it guilt or shame sabotaging your healing? Let's find out.

Grab your journal and go through this exercise step by step. Write it down—don't just think it.

1. **Separate Guilt from Shame**
   Ask yourself:

   - Do I feel responsible for surviving while others didn't? (That's guilt.)
   - Do I believe something is wrong with me for having PTSD? (That's shame.)
   - Write your answers honestly. Don't hold back.

2. **Complete These Prompts**

   - "The guilt I carry is…" (Finish this sentence until there's nothing left inside you.)
   - "The shame I carry is…" (Do the same here. Force it out of the shadows.)

3. **Name the Consequences**
   For each statement of guilt and shame you've written, ask:

   - What has this belief cost me? (Relationships? Opportunities? Peace?)

- What does it keep me from experiencing? (Connection? Joy? Freedom?)

4. **Challenge the Lie**
   Write:

- "The truth is..." and counter every statement of guilt and shame with what you know is real. Example: *"The guilt I carry is that I survived. The truth is I followed my orders, I fought with integrity, and my brothers would want me to live."*

5. **Commit to Honor**
   Write one final declaration:

- *"I honor the fallen not by suffering, but by living."* Say it out loud. Put it where you can see it. This is how you turn guilt into remembrance and shame into strength. What you expose, you can destroy.

YOUR HEALING KILLER AUDIT

It's time to take a brutal inventory. Look in the mirror and ask yourself— *which of the Healing Killers are fucking with my life?* Write them down. Right now.

If they persist, they will continue to block your healing and sabotage who you are meant to be. So let's get real and raw:

- What are these Healing Killers costing you?
- What price have you paid?
- What price is your family paying right now?

You're hiding out for hours at a time, numbing your pain instead of living. You run to the bottle, have put yourself in debt or watch pornography just to cope. Everyone tiptoes around you, afraid to set you off. You've lost relationships and have disconnected from reality.

I know this because I lived it. My wife walked on eggshells every single day, never knowing if she was going to get the calm version of me or the rage-fueled one. My kids saw me check out—physically there but emotionally gone—because I was drowning in numbing behaviors. I thought I was hiding it, but I wasn't. The alcohol, the avoidance—it poisoned the trust in my marriage and it shattered the way I saw myself as a husband and a father. To this day, some of that damage can never be erased. My wife still remembers the nights I disappeared instead of holding her. My kids still carry questions about why Dad wasn't really "there" when they needed him. That's what these Healing Killers cost me: the very relationships that I value the most in my life—the reason I fought to come home alive. That's the price I paid for letting them rule my life. And what kind of life was that anyway?

Now it's your turn to look in the mirror. This isn't about learning anymore. It's about reality—your reality.

Do you even feel alive? Or are you just a walking corpse—completely dead inside? Tolerating this bullshit ends now. What has this cost you? Your relationships? Your children? Your wife? Your income? Your freedom? Your businesses? Get real and face the truth. If nothing changes, where will you be six months from now? Will your kids speak to you? Will you still be stuck in the misery you feel now? Devoid of joy. Still stuck. Still numb. Still addicted. Your marriage shattered, your kids walking on eggshells, and your business plateaued. The same damn patterns, but worse.

Are you even still alive?

You must feel this now. *See it*. Feel all of it! Visualize what you are allowing to continue. Let this pain course through your body. Grit your teeth and stare that future in the face. Let your anger and intensity build.

Now, here's the critical transition: you already built leverage earlier in this book. You've already looked five and 10 years down the road and seen the destruction ahead if nothing changes. But this time is different. This time you're putting the spotlight directly on the Healing Killers themselves. This is about the addictions, the shame, the avoidance, the half-assed effort—the exact poisons you just identified in your own life.

So here's your mission: build leverage against each Killer specifically. Write it out. If I keep numbing, what happens to my marriage? If I keep isolating, what happens to my kids? If I keep wearing the "broken veteran" label, what happens to my identity?

This isn't a repeat exercise—it's a deeper strike. Earlier, you built leverage against the general future of doing nothing. Now, you are going target by target, Killer by Killer. You are making it impossible to tolerate even one of them staying in your life another day.

Because if you don't build leverage against each of these bastards individually and rip them out by the roots, nothing will change. So:

1. Write down every Healing Killer you carry.
2. For each one, write the cost. To your marriage, your children, your health, and your finances.
3. Then write down what will happen in one year if you don't eliminate them. Then do it for five years. Then ten.
4. Now write down this phrase in big bold letters:
   "I REFUSE TO LET THIS BE MY FUTURE."

Say it out LOUD. Now scream:
"IT'S TIME TO BE FREE!"
Again. Louder.

DESTRUCTION SOP FOR COMMON KILLERS

Now you're ready to destroy the *common killers,* the more subtle yet no less destructive habits that derail your healing and infect your life.

But hear this: don't attack blindly or without a pre-planned approach. *Use the right weapon for the right target.* Each Healing Killer demands a specific strategy. So let's break them down.

Step 1: Identify the Healing Killers and their Damage
Start with truth. Which common killers are you letting live inside you: numbing, isolation, faulty beliefs, toxic self-talk? Which ones are you tolerating? Take an accurate inventory.

Then go deeper:

- What is it already *doing* to you?

- What has it already *cost* you?

Use the same leverage-building questions from the previous section *for each one.* You must feel the pain. The anger. The reality.

Step 2: Identify Your Triggers
What causes it or sets it off? Pain? Sadness? Fear of weakness? Trace it back to the source. A childhood wound? Military conditioning? Understand the real root instead of just tackling the underlying symptoms.

Step 3: Build Massive Leverage
This is your fuel. Revisit your why, visualize the cost of failure and inaction for each and every Healing Killer. Then visualize what your life would be like *without* this Healing Killer? Anchor this to your vision of freedom. Let that energy drive you.

Step 4: Deploy Support

Don't fight this battle alone. Leverage accountability partners, coaches, and professionals. Call in your Battle Buddy. They will help you crush these opponents.

Step 5: Commit Publicly

It's time to commit with absolute certainty and dedication. Make a public declaration that you will annihilate these Healing Killers and then display it openly. Make it impossible to avoid. Burn the boats. There can be no retreat.

Step 6: Replace with Powerful Alternatives

Every Healing Killer exists because it somehow meets one of your core human needs—but in a destructive way. The problem isn't that you had the need; the problem is the toxic strategy you used to meet it. You cannot destroy a Healing Killer without replacing it with a stronger, empowering alternative that meets the same underlying need.

Here's how it plays out:

- **Certainty** (safety, comfort): Instead of alcohol to "calm down," train your body with routines, deep breathing, grounding drills, or progressive muscle relaxation. These give certainty without destruction.

- **Uncertainty/Variety** (stimulation, change): Instead of gambling or other risky behaviors, channel that drive into martial arts, adventure sports, or travel. Positive variety fuels growth, not destruction.

- **Significance** (feeling important, strong): Instead of rage or domination, lead your family, serve your community, or train your body. True significance comes from contribution and mastery.

- **Love/Connection**: Instead of porn or codependency, lean into genuine intimacy with your spouse, deeper friendships, or brotherhood in veteran communities.

- **Growth**: Instead of compulsive numbing, commit to a skill, read, or train. Growth builds power.

- **Contribution**: Instead of self-destruction, pour yourself into helping others, mentoring, or serving your fellow vets. Contribution heals shame and guilt faster than anything.

Step 7: Condition the New Behavior
It is crucial that you condition and reward your progress. Celebrate every win. You are rewiring your brain. Associate pain with the old behavior and pleasure (joy, peace, strength) to your replacement. This creates further leverage.

Step 8: Track Everything
Track your wins, challenges, what worked, and what didn't. If eating clean helps you love better, document it. This will help reinforce what works for you.

Step 9: Set Micro-Goals
You don't need to win this battle in one day. Just focus on each Healing Killer for an hour a day. Aim small and miss small. Set small intentions throughout the day. Then track and celebrate as discussed.

Step 10: Live Clean and Strong
Finally, live clean and take care of your body. I've said it before—physical health and mental health go hand in hand. Eat clean, hydrate, sleep well, and exercise daily. When you take care of your body you will have more energy, focus, and drive. This is foundational.

Remember that you're dealing with ingrained, reinforced, and conditioned patterns. But everything can be reconditioned and retrained *with the right tools*.

ASSAULT PLAN FOR ULTIMATE KILLERS

It's time to deploy precision tactics to destroy the Ultimate Killers: the numbing addictions and survivor's guilt.

NUMBING ADDICTIONS

First: Start with leverage. A true numbing addiction requires more leverage and focus than before. Go back to the leverage-building questions, but this time, make your answers 10 times more powerful. Whether it's alcohol, pornography, rage, or even adrenaline, it doesn't matter. All addictions follow the same neural pattern: pain ➡ trigger ➡ relief ➡ reinforcement. Break this loop and replace it.

You need to hate this addiction. Visualize the damage it has and will cause in the worst possible scenario. The lost relationships, wasted time, destroyed health, and moments missed with your family. Feel that anger, it will fuel you. Build the leverage until staying the same becomes more painful than breaking free. Without enough leverage, this is extremely difficult to do.

Second: Remove the source. Work smarter, not harder. Delete the gambling apps, throw away your alcohol, put adult blocks on your phone. Make access to your addiction extremely difficult. Involve an accountability partner to reinforce your approach.

Third: Ride the wave. Addictions are experienced with urges. These urges rise, peak, and fall like waves in the ocean. Train yourself to pause, breathe, and let the wave pass without giving in. Remember: an urge is just a sensation in your body, not a command. It will not kill you. It feels overwhelming because your nervous system has been wired to expect the old behavior, but like every wave, it will crest and fade if you don't act on it. Ride it out.

Fourth: Create a response plan. Know what you'll do *instead* when the trigger hits. Replace the behavior, don't just remove it. Chew gum, exercise, connect with your wife, or take a cold shower. You need a substitute to replace the underlying need. If you only try to cut the addictive behavior without replacing it, you'll create a vacuum—and your brain will drag you right back into the old habit. Every addiction meets a need, and if you rip the behavior away without a substitute, you haven't actually handled the underlying need. That's why you must plan ahead with replacements. Don't leave your brain empty-handed.

For some of you, the previous strategies alone won't be enough. Some addictions are deeply compulsive and require professional help. If you are battling alcohol, drugs, gambling, or any destructive behavior that feels bigger than you, get help immediately. This doesn't make you weak—it makes you lethal in the fight for your freedom. There are 12-Step programs, detox centers, rehab facilities, and specialized trauma therapists built to help you crush this. Use them. Don't let shame keep you trapped.

Fifth: Reward progress and stay connected. Celebrate every win with your Battle Buddy. Track your victories. Keep score. This will compound each win and maximize your momentum.

SHAME AND GUILT

Now to the other insidious killers: shame and guilt. Leverage is still crucial, but more emotional now. Reframe the killer first. You're not honoring your brothers, you're discrediting them. Understand what shame and guilt has cost you—connection, intimacy and energy. See the damage clearly and then ask yourself: *Would those I mourn want me to suffer? Is guilt actually helping me?* Of course not.

First: Reframe the meaning of your guilt and shame: Honor the memories of the fallen and yourself through how you live, not how you suffer. That's how you show gratitude.

Second: Cut the triggers. If dates, places, or songs pull you back into this darkness, remove these triggers. Acknowledge the feeling when it occurs, use grounding techniques, then shift your state to a more empowered one using your Triad.

Third: Release it. Write a letter to the brothers you lost. Put into words the guilt and shame you've been carrying for them. Tell them the truth: "I honor your sacrifice. I will never forget you, but I will no longer destroy myself. I choose to live, to heal, and to carry you forward in strength—not in endless suffering." Burn the letter. Hold your own goodbye ceremony. Speak it aloud: "Thank you. I honor your memory. But I no longer carry this pain."

Finally: Reframe to empowerment. Train yourself to think: "I feel this because I cared. But I'm done punishing and hurting myself." Recondition your nervous system to this truth. Declare it, embody it. Then, move forward.

OPERATION CLEAN SWEEP

You've now exposed the Healing Killers for what they are. You've seen how they sabotage your life, relationships, and mission. Now comes the decisive step: execution. Naming them isn't enough. Understanding them isn't enough. You must destroy them with a written, detailed battle plan. This isn't a suggestion—it's the bridge between knowledge and freedom. Go to the free resource page at *www.WarriorsAwakening. com/free-resources* and download the Healing Killers Plan of Attack worksheet. This is your campaign plan. Treat it like orders before combat: once written, you will follow it with unrelenting discipline until the enemy is gone. Here's how you'll create and execute your plan:

Step 1: Start with the Target
Get absolutely clear. Which killer(s) are you destroying with the chosen strategy? Be specific. Don't just write "stop drinking" or "no more

shame." Write: "I will eliminate nightly alcohol use by September 1st. I am going to replace this with my coping skills. When I feel the urge to drink, I will take a cold shower, journal my experience, and check-in with my partner. I will track this in my daily journal."

Every killer gets its own battle plan with clear deadlines, measurable goals, and real-world consequences.

Step 2: Revisit Your Leverage and Your Why
Yes, again. Until it's ingrained in your nervous system. It's time to face reality and accept the truth. What's the cost if you don't eliminate this? What's the freedom you gain if you do? Write it. Feel it. Revisit it.

Step 3: Choose Your Tools
Deploy the right tools for each killer. Plan ahead for your triggers. Remove access to your addictions. Use reframing and the ritual release for shame. Review the strategies and pick the right tools according to what you've learned. Then schedule their use.

Step 4: Plan for Reinforcement
What will you do daily to reinforce your new behaviors? Build your reinforcement strategies using rewards, self-praise, sharing of your victories, or ritual celebrations. Force your brain to crave these victories.

Step 5: Go Public
Make your commitment known. Tell your tribe. Post your plan where you (and others) will see it every day. Film a video of yourself declaring it out loud and watch it daily. Time to burn the boats. No retreat.

Step 6: Daily Conditioning
When dealing with addictions or deeply ingrained behaviors, the key is retraining your brain through consistent daily practice. When the urge rises, interrupt it with a phrase that re-centers you. Make it short,

sharp, and personal. Then immediately back it up with action: take the cold shower, go for the sprint, call your Battle Buddy. Words alone don't rewire you—words *with* decisive action do.

Step 7: Stay Vigilant

Healing killers don't die easily, so expect resistance. Expect them to resurface, especially in moments of challenge. Have your plan ready for when they do.

CHAPTER 11

THE IDEAL LIFE OFFENSIVE
DESIGNING AND LIVING YOUR FULL AND COMPLETE LIFE-LONG VICTORY

AFTER-ACTION REPORT

Before we move on, you need to take stock of what you've accomplished. First, revisit where you were at the very beginning of your journey. When you first opened this book, what were you feeling? Maybe it was desperation. Maybe you just wanted *relief* or weren't sure if healing was even possible. For most, the starting point was a simple, fragile thing: **hope**. Hope that you weren't broken. Hope that you could feel again. Hope that there was a way out.

Now look at where you are today and who you've become. How far have you come? Set a timer and write for 15 minutes in your journal. Feel the gratitude and honor your victories.

Ask yourself:

- What did I hope for when I started?
- What have I achieved since then?

- What damaging beliefs have I destroyed?

- What powerful habits have I built?

- How has my identity changed?

Get out your journal and write this down. Don't skip this step. It's crucial that you see your progress, summarize your learning points, and reinforce your growth if you want true change. When you intentionally and consciously reflect on your progress, you create emotional certainty that you are progressing as needed toward victory.

While you're at it, revisit your gratitude. What are you grateful for now that you weren't before? What moments, victories, or insights would have been impossible without this journey? Give yourself space to *feel* that.

Here's what I know: if you've done the work in this book, really *done it,* then you've already changed your life and are on a new trajectory. Not in theory. In reality.

Now it's time to shift your focus from short-term relief to long-term purpose and planning. When most veterans begin this work, their vision rarely extends past tomorrow or next month. They just want to stop the pain. But you've stopped it. Now it's time to build the very thing you fought so hard for—your life.

The next phase is building and living your Ideal Life Plan. No more "reacting"; it's time to rewrite the rest of your life. Your ideal life—one that fulfills, empowers, and energizes you and reflects the new identity you've created.

You're no longer the same man who started this book, you are the badass motherfucker you were destined to be.

THE VISION BEFORE THE PLAN: CRAFTING YOUR IDEAL LIFE PLAN

You've broken PTSD. It's ass has been kicked. The symptoms that once dictated your days are either gone or under your complete control as you continue to retrain and condition your nervous system. Your identity has shifted. Your habits, your rules, and your motivations are all being rewired. You're not just surviving to avoid the pain anymore— you're living free.

It's time to build your Ideal Life Plan—the blueprint for the next chapter. This isn't just theory. This is about building a future that promotes your growth, amplifies your power, and fuels your purpose and fulfillment.

First, you must get clear on where you're going. To create this plan, you need absolute clarity. Clarity requires absolute certainty. This certainty will fuel your execution. Without a crystal-clear vision, you'll drift. You'll waste time and may get frustrated about your lack of progress. You'll potentially relapse into old patterns. You'll feel unsettled without the chaos you've grown so used to. You need something bigger to move toward, and that is your Ideal Life Plan.

Here's how it works.

IDEAL LIFE PLAN EXERCISE

Get into a quiet space. Close your eyes and center yourself. Breathe deeply and relax. Now visualize your life 20 years from now.

Answer the following, in your journal:

1. Who are you?
2. What does your identity look like now that PTSD is behind you? What do you stand for?

3. What are you doing?

4. Describe your daily life. Your work. Your health. Your relationships. What are you building each and every day? Who do you spend your time with? What are you focusing on creating?

5. Where are you?

6. Where do you live? What do you see when you wake up each morning? Describe your environment.

7. What are you known for?

8. How do people describe you? How are you remembered? What legacy are you building? What contributions are you making?

9. What do you feel?

10. What are your base feelings and emotions? Are you calm? Energized? Overflowing with love, joy, and peace?

11. What have you achieved?

12. What have you accomplished? What have you built? What goals are completed?

Once you have done this for 20 years from now, do it for 10 and five years respectively.

Use every sense. *See it. Hear it. Smell it. Touch it.* This is no vague dream. This is your life unfolding in front of you. This *has* actually occurred. Now write it out, *in the present tense*, as if you already have it. Because if you want to build it, you need to feel and believe it.

Don't write: "I want to be happier." Write: "I wake up every day with joy and purpose. My family feels it. My business reflects it. My life proves it." Be specific and measurable. If you can't objectively track it, you can't build it.

This vision is now the foundation for your Ideal Life Plan in the next section. Without it, you're building randomly. With it, every decision will be a building block toward this achieved outcome.

Also remember to state your PTSD in the past tense. Say it out loud: "I used to have PTSD. I no longer do." You are not the same man who began this book. You've transformed. And now it's time to declare who you will become next.

LOCKING IN LEVERAGE

You now have your Ideal Life Plan. It's clear. It's powerful. But vision alone doesn't get the job done. Desire does.

You've used leverage multiple times already. It's what got you to this point. Leverage keeps you motivated and committed when times are challenging. You tapped into a mixture of pain avoidance and pleasure seeking to break PTSD's grip. You relied on the vision of who you wanted to become combined with your new identity. Now you'll use that same power again, this time not for the destruction of PTSD, but to create your long-term future.

Creating this next chapter of your life demands even greater direction, desire, and intensity. Your goals are bigger, the changes more substantial, your timeline is longer, and the chances of distraction are greater. So this requires an even greater anchor, with even more motivation, and that's where this next exercise comes in. You must fuel this next phase of your life with a reason so powerful, you'll fight through anything to achieve it.

Let's make something clear first: you always *could* have built this life. The only thing missing was the roadmap and the internal shift. You now have both. That means there are no more excuses. There's only the question: *Why must I create this life? Why will I stop at nothing to have it?*

Pull out your Ideal Life Plan again. Reread it and ask yourself: *Why does this matter so deeply to me?*

This is about more than *you*. This is about your family, your legacy, and everything you will accomplish. It's about being the father, husband, son, leader, and warrior you were born to be—free of the prison you created. It's about choosing to build something meaningful.

LEVERAGE EXERCISE: BUILD YOUR "WHY"

In your journal, answer these questions with full intensity. Don't hold back.

1. Why do I *need* to live this Ideal Life?
2. If I don't achieve this, what will it cost me emotionally, financially, spiritually?
3. Who will suffer if I quit and give up?
4. Who will benefit if I go all in?
5. What will it feel like to wake up in this Ideal Life every day?
6. Why will I stop at *nothing* to create this Life?

Then write a paragraph about your Ideal Life in the present tense—not as a vision of the future, but as a declaration of the present. Earlier you wrote about your future life as something you were aiming for. Now you are locking it in as if it already **exists**, because identity is lived in the *now*. Write as though you already embody it. This isn't about hoping—it's about owning it.

Finally, revisit or remake your Battle Board. This time, you're not adding "healing goals." Those battles are done. Now your board must reflect empowerment, contribution, fulfillment, and legacy. Replace every old symbol of survival with new images of the life you are already living. Make it so clear and compelling that every time you see it, your nervous system says: *This is who I am*. Then revisit it daily.

This is how you shift from healing to building and living the masterpiece of your life.

FROM VISION TO BLUEPRINT

It's time to turn your Ideal Life Plan into a workable blueprint. We will do this by breaking it into smaller, tactical objectives you can effectively execute. This will make your Plan clear, objective, and obtainable.

Big objectives without a smaller defined structure can be overwhelming, leading to delays and frustration. But when we *chunk* (thanks, Tony Robbins) the vision into simple, clear milestones, anything can be accomplished. That's how we operated in the military. We didn't stare at the entire mission and freeze. We broke it down: move here, clear this, secure that. Simplicity wins battles.

Your long-term life plan must follow the same rule. It needs to be simple, trackable, and broken into manageable units of time and outcomes. Why? Because even the clearest long-term vision gets overwhelming when it is too general and complex. But a 12-month goal with exact outcomes for each week? That's a target you can take down.

If you're more of a longer-term operator, that's fine. Break it down into one-year, three-year, five-year, 10-year, and 20-year intervals. Then reverse-engineer your long-range goal into daily action steps. If you love shorter targets, then break it into regularly repeating smaller pieces that are easy to track and attack daily.

This concept, called chunking, will prevent you from becoming overwhelmed by keeping you engaged in regular, trackable goals and specific targets, one step at a time.

Go back to your Ideal Life Plan and answer these questions:

- How do I want to feel every day?
- Who do I want to be?
- What do I want to experience?
- What do I want to accomplish?
- Where do I want to go, live, or travel?
- What do I want to build?
- What legacy do I want to leave?
- What relationships do I want to deepen or create?

Break each of your answers from the list above into specific, objective, and measurable categories:

- Mental and Physical Health
- Business, Wealth, and Financial Freedom
- Adventure, Travel, and Experiences
- Relationships and Family
- Contribution, Spirituality, and Impact

Then break down your measurable categories into clear objectives, each with small steps and individual targets. These smaller objectives should have weekly or at least monthly outcomes that then lead into the one-year, three-year, five-year, 10-year, and 20-year blocks.

Once that multistep breakdown is done, build an accountability tool to track your success. This could be a spreadsheet or something similar to help you track your progress each week, month, or year.

Tracking accomplishes two things: it manifests progress and reinforces successes. If you track your targets, you'll see the trends. Once you see them, you'll feel their momentum and energy, which, then, drives you forward and prompts you to repeat them. Do you want to track your wealth? Use financial milestones. Your mental health? Do weekly mood check-ins. Want to improve your physical health? Track weekly weight and strength targets.

This is how you create the life you were born to live. Not all at once, but strategically over time. If you've ever built a business, this strategy should feel familiar. Clear performance indicators, targets, and regular financial reviews. To dominate your life, the model is no different. Your life, family, and health all deserve the same level of clarity and structure. Don't leave your best life to chance.

ASSIGNMENT 19: From vision to blueprint.

Perform each of the following steps and write the answers down clearly in your journal.

1. Review your Ideal Life Plan.
2. Break your overall targets into clear, measurable goals across one, three, five, 10, and 20 years.
3. Create monthly tracking systems for each category.
4. Start executing. Then track and reinforce.

This is how you turn vision into reality to achieve your ideal life.

FULL SYSTEMS INTEGRATION

This is it. You've built your Ideal Life Plan, chunked it into targets, and armed yourself with the tools to reprogram pain, control emotions, and execute your daily plans. You have a new life now and a clear plan to make it happen.

From this moment forward, you live deliberately, with intention, desire, and fulfillment—not in reaction, but by design. *Your* design.

Now, take everything you've written:

- Your Vision

- Your "Why"

- Your Tactical Objectives

- Your one-, three-, five-, 10-, and 20-year goals

- Your tracking systems

And combine them into a single, structured Ideal Life Plan. This is your battle plan for a life of total freedom, power, peace, purpose, and fulfillment. For you, your kids, and your spouse.

Even the most beautifully written plan is worthless without ruthless, relentless, daily action. You know this now. You must now become a relentless force in pursuit of your plans. Don't wait for perfection, don't hesitate, just execute. Obliterate your obstacles. If there's no way forward, create one.

Win or win. Victory or victory. No compromises.

If PTSD symptoms ever creep back in—a new trigger, memory, or wave of emotion—don't worry. In fact, anticipate this. You're not broken, you are human and you are now prepared. You have all the tools you need to identify them, tolerate them, and crush them. You're no longer at the mercy of your nervous system. You are powerful and completely free.

But freedom requires constant maintenance. Just like in combat, no plan survives first contact unchanged. Rounds come down range, the terrain shifts, and you must adapt. The same is true here—your healing and freedom plan must be reassessed, tested, and refined. If you don't adapt, you risk slipping back into old patterns. Anticipate this reality and stay relentless.

Here's how to maintain your edge:

1. Finalize Your Ideal Life Plan

Bring everything together—your identity, your values, your new beliefs, your conditioning strategies, and your long-term vision—into one clearly written document. This will become your field manual for living. Don't leave it scattered across random notes. Consolidate it into one place you can reference daily. If you haven't done this yet, do this now.

2. Track with Precision

Every warrior tracks their weapons, ammo, and supplies. You must track your progress with the same intensity.

- *Physical health:* Record weight, strength, endurance, and consistency with training.

- *Mental/emotional health:* Use mood logs, energy ratings, and quick reflections on your connection with family and friends.

- *Emotional baseline:* Note your most common state. If it isn't gratitude, peace, and power—then it's time to retrain.

- *Goal Progress:* Record your progress toward each of your Ideal Life Plan goals regularly.

- *Reinforce Your Vision:* Your brain forgets fast. That's why you must reinforce it every day. Read your life plan weekly. Visualize it daily. Speak your identity and commitments out loud with intensity until they are encoded into your nervous system. Make it impossible to forget who you are, where you are going, all the progress you have made, and *why* it all matters so much to you.

- *Adapt Ruthlessly:* If something isn't working, don't sit in self-pity or denial—adjust. Replace what fails with a better strategy. Life changes—new stressors appear, new challenges arise, and new seasons pass. Adapt your plan to stay aligned with your mission.

- *Commit to Lifelong Growth:* Freedom isn't a one-time victory— it's a way of life. Keep moving forward. Build new goals, stretch into new missions, and never stop growing. Stagnation is the enemy. Growth is your weapon and who you are now.

Your Final Drill: Condition the Forever Life Plan and stand tall. Loudly declare: "This is my life. I built it. I chose it. It is mine. I will live it."

CHAPTER 12

THE LONG GAME
SUSTAINING VICTORY FOR LIFE

THE FORWARD WARRIOR MINDSET

You've reached the end of the initial phase of your journey with me. You have a plan for your ideal life, with everything that you need to accomplish it, and the strategies to crush whatever obstacles come your way. This chapter is about maintaining what you've built.

It's time to embody the Forward Warrior Mindset.

The Forward Warrior Mindset is about never again retreating into the past. It's the discipline of advancing, no matter the terrain. You've fought through the darkness, rebuilt yourself, and reclaimed control, but the mission isn't over. Warriors don't stand still—they adapt, evolve, and drive forward every day with clarity and purpose. This mindset is the embodiment of vigilance, growth, and leadership. It's about being proactive instead of reactive, deliberate instead of adrift, powerful instead of passive. Warriors don't wait for peace—they create it. They carry their mission into every day, every moment, every breath.

Remember this: Freedom isn't a one-time victory. It's a life-long campaign. Your journey for peace will continue every single day—not because you're broken, but because you are alive and evolving. Every sunrise is another chance to lead yourself, to choose strength, and to live the identity you've built. True warriors don't retire from the battlefield—they adapt, rearm, and stay sharp. Then you will have the opportunity to lead others to do the same.

But now, it's time to stack successes and recognize your progress and wins. Praise yourself. Feel that success and train your nervous system in the process.

ASSIGNMENT 20: Reflecting on your progress and wins.

Reflect (again) on how far you've come. In your journal now, write down five to 10 wins for which you can be truly grateful. These should make you swell with pride. Really feel it and enjoy it as you write down each word.

You've trained your mind, rewired your nervous system, and rebuilt your life from the inside out. Now, your mission is maintenance and mastery. The same intensity that once fueled your fight out of the darkness must now fuel your consistency. It's not about grand victories anymore—it's about the daily disciplines, the quiet moments of choice, and the relentless execution of everything you've learned.

By consistently deploying these strategies with Absolute Commitment, you will continue to experience your freedom for the rest of your life. Go to the free resource page at *www.WarriorsAwakening.com/free-resources* and download your Forward Warrior Maintenance Checklist to help you organize and keep driving forward every day.

You will never return to where you were when you started this journey. Remember: you are not who you were when this began. That version of you is buried.

BROTHERHOOD AND BEYOND

To maintain your freedom, two strategies stand above the rest: community and connection.

Every veteran knows the strength of a unit. In the military, our brothers had our back. We were stronger together. This gave us safety, purpose, and relentless drive when we fought together. You felt unstoppable with them, but mostly, you understood and connected to them. You need that again.

Now, nothing will ever replicate your unit from the sandbox or the jungle, but we can still leverage this strategy. Being part of a community that not only understands you, but will hold you accountable and maintain your momentum is invaluable. You need a new brotherhood: one that will lift you up, challenge you, and push you forward. But beware: not all veteran groups are created equal. Many so-called "support groups" will do the opposite. They will hurt you and drag you back to where they are. They bond over pain and suffering, embracing "the suck" they identify with. They will tell you healing isn't possible. They wear their symptoms as a badge of honor.

These are the Healing Killers you've destroyed.

I've been in those rooms. I've heard "this is just how life is now." We shouldn't blame them because they've been indoctrinated into the old way of thinking: "We will never heal. This is who we are." I also believed it once. If you enter a group like this, leave it. Protect yourself and do not absorb their mental poison. Instead, seek a group that ignites growth, challenges you, and will see you forward. If that sounds rare, it is. But I've found it. I actually created it for my Combat Veteran Clients solely for this purpose. You can find one too. Feel free to check out my website for more information about my veteran community as well.

Connection is about you becoming the teacher. When you teach what you've learned, you'll move your knowledge from theory to application. You're no longer just a student—you help your comrades deploy what you've learned, which simultaneously builds clarity, execution, and consistency for yourself.

I went through this process when I began writing this book. I couldn't just know the strategies: I had to live them. And I did, because I was now responsible for transferring these tools to my veteran community. So find a veteran brother and teach them these strategies. It will produce faster growth in you too.

Here's your task:

1. Join a community that builds you up.
2. Teach someone what you've learned.

These two tools are simple but potent. They'll reinforce everything you've learned and drive you forward with relentless momentum.

CONTINUING CONDITIONING

The next strategy for sustainable freedom is to continue your conditioning. Like I've said, conditioning is crucial—not just for rewiring yourself, but for creating your new automatic muscle memory as well.

Think back to when you joined the military. Everything—your uniform, posture, and weapon—was foreign. But your leaders conditioned you through repetition until it all became pure instinct. You didn't think when you cleared a room. You reacted from your training: Clear door, buttonhook right followed by your brother who hooked left. Breach, clear, secure. Did you have to ponder how to hold your rifle? Of course not. You were a trained and conditioned machine.

This is no different.

But that level of automatic response required hundreds of hours of training. Imagine if you applied that level of discipline to your life now. To create automatic responses, the same discipline you had back then is required. But this time, it's about your emotions, identity, habits, and internal responses. Just like your combat unit conditioned clearing rooms, this new training must condition your emotional readiness.

When I got promoted from lance corporal to corporal, I knew I wasn't ready. I was timid and unsure. But my leaders were confident, certain, and composed under pressure. I had no choice: I had to become confident. So I reverse-engineered it. I broke it down into behavior: how did a Confident Corporal walk, look, speak, and hold himself? Then I simply modeled and held myself the same way, every minute of every day. I didn't feel confident or like a leader... not yet. Shoulders back. Eyes sharp. Breath deep. Voice strong. Muscles tense. Every single conversation, I executed the identity of a Confident Corporal. Little did I know the power of what I was doing. And then something happened: Suddenly I was one. The repetition became forged into my body. That version of me has never left.

Gentlemen, it's going to take immense repetition to create the muscle memory and automatic responses you need. This is your new normal. Don't wait to "feel like it." This is now your daily existence.

Your Daily Assignment

1. Condition your new identity every day with your very posture, breath, words, and physical presence.

2. Repeat your power incantations and belief shifts regularly.

3. Celebrate every win to reinforce the changes.

4. Never stop. Repetition is the mother of all mastery. Conditioning is the path to permanent freedom.

This is how the new you becomes the only you.

YOUR FINAL OATH

The final strategies I have for you will teach you the power of continuing your commitment and the power of recommitting, especially when you are crushing addictions, old patterns, and old habits.

Victory against previously entrenched and conditioned opponents demands daily recommitment, especially in the early stages of healing when old habits, addictions, and coping mechanisms try to pull you back. Your brain was trained for years. Change is scary and your brain will resist, but you can easily overcome this discomfort with the skills you've learned. But it will require staying committed by deploying regular recommitment strategies. Without your intense commitment, the energy and dedication you feel now won't last.

You're not broken or failing when you falter. You're just being given an opportunity to grow stronger. This is how ultimate life-long victory occurs: Daily commitment. Study the challenge. Learn from the outcome and then adjust. Once you've adjusted, recommit again and condition the strategy.

You will not relent. You will not back down. Your vision, your outcome, the ideal life that you have planned for requires this continued commitment. You have done this many times so far—time to do it again. And again. And again. Make your declaration out loud. Do it over and over, louder and louder. Involve your body. Pound your chest, stomp your feet, jump up in the air, scream, yell, pump your hands in the air. Success or success. Declare this publicly. Journal your wins. Recognize your successes. Deploy your community as a powerful resource.

Old friends may not understand. Family members may resist. They know the old you. Some of them even prefer the broken version—because your pain made them feel better about their own. If you stay stuck, they never have to face their demons. If you rise, it forces them to see what's possible, and that terrifies them. They might mock your efforts, question your healing, or even try to pull you back into old habits. That's not your concern. Love them, but don't let their limiting beliefs—or their comfort in your suffering—stop your drive. You're not here to make them comfortable. You're here to reclaim your freedom.

Finally, hear this and never forget it:

- Your healing is not linear.
- You will have challenging days.
- You will mess up.

So what? Get up. Recommit and refocus. Every challenge is your opportunity to grow. Welcome them.

This is who you are now.

Your Final Orders:

1. Recommit daily, especially when it's hard.
2. Expect those around you to not understand and oppose your growth (especially family that don't like this "new you").
3. Never lose focus of your why and your vision.
4. Celebrate and reinforce your wins.
5. Anticipate opposition and keep attacking.
6. Declare your new self, again and again.

You are committed. You are unstoppable. You are free. *Forever*.

A NOTE FROM ME TO YOU

Thank you for trusting me to guide you through this journey. I hope you have all the tools you need now to continue to win and live your best life—free from PTSD and its symptoms forever.

Remember, you are not broken. You are in control.

You have the power to heal yourself whenever you choose to; you have the power to completely rewrite your life and crush PTSD forever and start living the life that you deserve. Remember your life does not have to be this way. Whenever you feel yourself struggling, you can choose to deploy the strategies that you have learned and live free.

I encourage you and welcome you to reach out to me. You can have the freedom that you've always wanted.

You never know what the purpose might be for the challenges that you faced and the obstacles that you overcame.

So keep up the good fight, keep pushing, take the hill. You will win.

If I hadn't gone through this journey, I wouldn't be teaching you this now. So thank you for joining me. It's been an honor to help you achieve the freedom you were born to live.

ABOUT THE AUTHOR

David Shoup is a United States Marine Corps combat veteran who served as an infantry rifleman in support of Operation Iraqi Freedom along with numerous other related duties such as a Special Operations Supporting Unit in various locations. After leaving active duty, he began a relentless personal mission: to destroy his PTSD and reclaim the life he was meant to live. David wrestled with nightmares, rage, anxiety, isolation, and emotional chaos. But he refused to accept that this was "just how life is now," despite being told this by numerous combat veteran support groups. Through years of intensive study, high-level coaching, and mission-focused action, he built a proven system rooted in psychological science, cutting-edge neurological strategies, and raw battlefield-related strategies.

Now, David leads a national movement to eliminate PTSD from the lives of combat veterans and active-duty military members—forever. As a coach, speaker, author, and fellow combat veteran, he serves our nation's heroes who feel lost, broken, or stuck in perpetual survival mode. He speaks their language because he lived it. His system isn't therapy—it's an operational manual for complete freedom. His methodology will allow any veteran or active-duty military member to achieve not only hope for a fulfilled life but life-long freedom from PTSD. David is here to lead those who are ready to fight back, take their freedom, and live with power, clarity, and purpose again.

To connect with David and learn more about his work, visit his website at *www.WarriorsAwakening.com* and connect with him on Instagram at @Mission.Freedom.0311 and on Facebook @Mission.Freedom.0311.

FREE RESOURCES

To download your free resources for *Mission: Freedom*, please scan the QR code below: